ANXIETY AS AN ALLY

HOW I TURNED A WORRIED MIND INTO MY BEST FRIEND

BY DAN RYCKERT

@2015 Up To Something Publishing

Introduction

I'm as far removed from being a doctor as a human being can possibly be. I went to college for the most slacker-y of slacker majors (Film Studies), and it still took me five and a half years to actually get a degree. After graduating, I went on to early jobs at a local television station and a GPS company before eventually landing dream jobs where I play video games and talk about them for a living. None of my educational or vocational history points towards expert knowledge of the workings of the human mind, but a couple of pesky psychological conditions taught me that I better learn more about them if I didn't want to become a victim of them.

While I'm not a doctor, my 12-year battle with panic disorder and generalized anxiety disorder (along with a fun sprinkling of OCD and ADHD) has placed me in offices with many of them. I've been tested by MDs, spent countless hours speaking with psychologists, sat in chairs with needles in my head, tried various medications and herbal supplements, joined mental health message boards, discussed my problems with support groups, and tried many more things in the relentless pursuit of understanding and easing my anxious mind. Without a doubt, it has been the most difficult thing I've ever been through in my life.

Despite this, I sit here in 2015 happier and more successful than I've ever been. It's taken a dozen years, but all of those different approaches I've tried have left me with an assortment of techniques and reminders that keep me sane, healthy, and optimistic. I have a job that's been my dream since I was nine years old. I have a positive disposition that's virtually never compromised. For at least half a decade now, each year of my life has been significantly more enjoyable and fulfilling than its predecessor. In an odd way, I owe much of if not most of this to my struggle with anxiety.

It's a safe bet that many of you are familiar with my work online, whether it's from Giant Bomb, Game Informer, or Twitter. On the internet, I rarely speak up about serious subjects. Discussing things like my anxiety issues can be tricky, and it takes me out of my comfort zone. That's part of why I'm writing this book. Identifying something that scares you and tackling it headfirst regardless is one of the many approaches that I've found to help. Because of this, I've turned my initial hesitance to talk about this subject into a reason that I have to write it. Talking about these issues is an important step to recovery, and I hope that reading about my experiences and successes in the realm of anxiety disorders will be of help to others that haven't yet attained a firm grasp on them.

Most of this book is a chronological history of my experience with anxiety disorders. It starts with my first panic attack in 2003, and moves on to cover my college years of struggling to find ways to combat panic disorder and generalized anxiety disorder. Later, you'll learn about my slow realization of which methods worked for me and which didn't. My years of experimenting with a variety of remedies eventually paid off, as the strategies I taught myself prepared me for my jobs in the gaming industry. In the final chapters, I'll break down my most important tips for quick reference.

It took me twelve years to get to this point of having a relatively anxiety-free life. I hope that by discussing how I got here, I can provide some tips on how to accelerate your own process of eliminating anxiety. Your solutions may differ from mine, but this book will give examples of positive mindsets and methods that should apply to anyone even if my path isn't exactly the same as yours. In addition, I hope that this is a book that you can give to family and friends that struggle to understand what it's like to live with anxiety disorders.

Anxiety is a chronic condition. At no point in my life can I climb a hill and confidently yell "It's over!" It will be with me until the day I die, but I've learned how to harness it as a positive force instead of being burdened by the difficulties it comes with. It's my hope that as you read this book, you'll identify with many of these struggles and find benefit from the same approaches that have changed my life for the better.

The Beginning

My full-blown anxiety disorders didn't go into effect until a specific moment at the beginning of 2003, but evidence of me being a high-strung kid had long been present. I was socially awkward throughout all of my pre-college schooling, leading to plenty of name-calling and punches being thrown my way for years. I was a kid that was obsessed with video games and professional wrestling, couldn't talk to a girl to save my life, and never went to any school functions or parties. This wasn't unique to me, as it's a common story among many kids whether they were destined to develop anxiety disorders or not.

Despite never feeling fully comfortable in these early years, I had never experienced a panic attack, nor had I any knowledge of them. While my first panic attack was still months away, I entered a college preparatory program in the summer of 2002 with a great deal of nervousness. I had graduated high school in May of that year, and my mother convinced me to enroll in a one-month "Freshman Summer Institute" program that would prepare me for the full transition to come in the fall. It was a bite-sized version of a real college semester, requiring me to live in the dorms and attend a couple of summer classes.

This was my first time being forced out of my long-established comfort zone of playing video games at home on a near-nightly basis, and I can't say I handled it particularly well. I lived on campus in Lawrence, Kansas, which was only half an hour from my childhood home in Olathe. It may have been a stone's throw from the familiarity of home, but the forced social interaction made it feel like I might as well have been stationed in Siberia. Within a week, I was pacing in the lobby of the dorms, explaining to my parents on the phone that I had nothing in common with my peers. They drank and smoked pot, they listened to music I didn't like, and yet they all seemed happy to be there and had an instant kinship with each other. In retrospect, they probably harbored many of the anxieties I felt at that pivotal moment in our lives, but they did a much better job of hiding it. In my mind, I didn't belong there and I dreaded the years to come as I continued transitioning into the real world.

Early on, I found respite in the two classes that I was enrolled in. I never really enjoyed sitting in classrooms (and that feeling intensified as time went on), but it was a setting that I was at least familiar with. One was a basic introduction to the university and college life, and the other was Psychology 101. The latter was taught by a friendly, middle-aged professor named Buddy, and I hung around after most classes to chat with him. As a kid, I always felt more comfortable speaking with adults than with those my own age, and that had apparently carried over into (almost) adulthood. He always struck me as a genuinely happy person, so I enjoyed hearing his thoughts on life and how the mind works.

Because of Buddy's obvious intelligence and positive disposition, I gave something a chance that I normally wouldn't have. One day in class, he started talking to us about meditation. I knew nothing about it, and had always just assumed it was some pseudo-religious thing that hippies did while repeating weird chants. But because of how much I respected Buddy, I temporarily shut down the "this is a bunch of hippie crap" alarm that was blaring in my head, and I gave it a shot. He had the entire class close their eyes, and guided us through a simple meditation for ten minutes. He instructed us to focus on our breath as it moved in and out, and had us direct it to specific parts of our body in sequence (feet, calves, thighs, stomach, etc).

This is all very basic Meditation 101 stuff, but it was new to me at the time and was completely different than I expected. There was no chanting, no mantras, no praying to some god that I had never heard of — just breathing. He had a way of making it easy for even a class full of first-timers to fully focus on his instructions, and rarely did I find my mind wandering for those ten minutes. At the end, he instructed us to open our eyes and note how we felt. Even though I had yet to experience panic attacks or generalized anxiety, I noticed a distinct calm once the meditation was complete. I was floored by the feeling, and I remember Buddy saying "Note how you all feel after just ten minutes. If you do this for an hour a day, it will change your life. I promise you."

As impressed as I was by the effects of the ten minutes, I didn't continue to do it after that class. I felt like learning how to talk to girls was a more pressing issue in my life, but that still seemed too daunting so I stuck with the safety of video games in my free time. The ensuing months played out in predictable fashion. I remained unsure of how much I liked this new college life, but was slowly coming around to the idea of meeting like-minded new friends in this new environment. I started playing video games with my door open, and would even walk in to other rooms and introduce myself when I noticed other people doing the same.

Gaming became the common ground for me and many others on the floor, and my social anxiety was becoming less of an issue on a weekly basis. Before long, I was printing up flyers for a Soul Calibur tournament and putting them up all over campus. I went from hating the idea of socializing with my peers in the summer to gathering dozens of them in front of a TV and a Dreamcast in the dorm lobby by the end of 2002. Things were changing quickly, and I was actually starting to like college.

My first panic attack was on New Year's Day, 2003. It's very clear to me now that it was a panic attack, but as an 18 year-old kid with no previous knowledge of them, it was one of the most terrifying experiences of my life. I was fairly hung over after a fun New Year's Eve with some newfound friends (I'd learn the hangover/anxiety connection years later), and we went to see *Gangs of New York*. I had seen hundreds of movies in the theater, even spending four years working at an AMC prior to college and seeing just about everything that came out during that period. I'd usually sit dead center in the row to get the best view of the screen, as I did on this night. It was a holiday and the movie had only been out less than two weeks, so it was a packed house.

Near the end of the 160-minute running time of the film, I started feeling woozy and noticed a tingling sensation in my extremities. It was near the end of the movie, and I was getting pretty into it, so I initially chalked it up to excitement. As Leonardo DiCaprio and Daniel Day-Lewis fought during the climax, I could tell that something much worse was happening. The most frustrating part was, I couldn't place where this sudden feeling of complete dread was coming from.

I started sweating and placed my head in my hands, and my feet began to tap involuntarily. My breathing and heart rate became rapid, and my body and mind just couldn't take it any more. Despite being really into the movie for the previous two and a half hours, everything inside of me was suddenly screaming that I had to get out of the room. I was even too rattled to feel like a jerk as I scooted past everyone in my row, obstructing their view during a pivotal scene.

I rushed into the bathroom with no real intention other than getting away from people. Hurrying into an open stall, I shut the door behind me and immediately started dry heaving into the toilet. My stomach felt fine, but my mind decided that dry heaving was the way to deal with this situation for some reason. Producing nothing, I wound up sitting on the toilet fully clothed and resting my head in my hands again as I tried to steady my erratic breathing. I was sweating profusely at this point, and more scared than I had ever been in my entire life. This wasn't "feeling sick," this was feeling like I was about to die at any moment from some unknown cause.

When I felt composed enough to face people again, I went to the sink and splashed some water on my face, then exited the bathroom. My friends were waiting outside, and were understandably wondering what the hell was wrong with me. I had left during the climax of a movie, and I was covered in sweat and clearly rattled the next time they saw me. I remember muttering something about feeling sick or hung over, and said I just needed to go home and rest a bit.

While it was a terrible and confusing night, I told myself that it was nothing more than a freak occurrence. My body felt fine when I woke up the next morning, and my mind wasn't giving off any red flags that anything was wrong. I continued as normal for the next week of the long holiday break (our school didn't start up again until three weeks into January), and nothing flared up.

A week after seeing *Gangs of New York*, I ventured back into the theater to see an even longer movie, *The Lord of the Rings: The Two Towers*. It was the same seating situation at the same theater with the same group of friends, but I didn't go in with any real worries of a repeat of the incident that occurred just a week prior.

In almost the exact same situation, the feelings of dread popped up near the end. The same shallow breathing, the same rapid heart rate, the same sweaty face and palms. Again, I rushed out of the theater and took refuge in the same bathroom stall.

This is where I really started to worry, as it surely wasn't a coincidence. Why did this feeling seem to overtake my body twice, in the exact same situation? Was I doomed to miss the climax of every movie for the rest of my life so that I could sit on the toilet for mysterious reasons? I was far from an expert on medical issues, but I had never even heard of anything like what I was experiencing.

I reacted in the worst possible way – by going home and spending the entire night searching the internet for answers about what could possibly be wrong with me. At one point, I thought I had Lyme disease. At others, I was convinced that I had any number of rare neurological disorders. When nothing seemed to be an obvious answer, I settled on a particularly ominous one – *I must be going crazy.*

Lying in bed that night, it was impossible to quiet my mind. I've had trouble sleeping throughout my entire life, but this was on a level that I had never experienced. The sun came up without me getting a single minute of sleep, and I was frequently hopping out of bed to do more fruitless internet searches throughout the night and morning.

Making the situation worse the next day was the fact that I was afraid to tell my mother about it. Growing up, she had always been easy to approach and very helpful whenever I had questions, concerns, or just needed someone to talk to. That said, this seemed like a very different beast. I knew I could turn to her for motherly advice on how to ask a girl out or how I should prepare for college, but "Mom, I think I might be going crazy" seemed like a much taller order for a conversation.

Within a couple of days, a combination of factors likely led to me becoming very sick. I'd have to imagine that the lack of sleep and the extreme amounts of mental stress had done a physical number on my body. Not only was I not sleeping, I was so stressed that I wasn't even getting hungry. For days, I'd barely eat as I alternated between laying in bed with a racing mind and scouring the internet for any information I could find. Late at night, I frequently found myself dry-heaving in the bathroom due to panic, but there was rarely any food in my stomach.

One of these nights, my mother heard me loudly dry-heaving and came to check on me.

"Party a bit too hard tonight?" she asked from the bathroom doorway.

"No, I just think I'm really sick," I responded.

"Surrre," she said. "You know, you're 18. As long as you're being safe about everything, you don't have to hide it from me if you've been drinking."

I initially wanted to explain to her that I hadn't had a drop, but decided that her thinking I was drunk was a better alternative to thinking her son was insane.

After days of worsening symptoms (mental and physical), I decided that I had to go to the doctor. I'd avoid talking about the mental aspects that scared me the most, and see if the doctor could find something physically wrong with me that would explain what was happening.

When my appointment started, I began with my best explanation of the physical symptoms. I told him that I had been feeling feverish and fatigued, with odd tingling sensations in my extremities and an occasional sensation that made me feel like I needed to vomit. As I explained this, the very symptoms I described came down on me like an avalanche. My breathing and heart rate spiked faster than ever, and the doctor could tell something was wrong. He told me to lie down on the table immediately, and ran out of the room to grab a nurse and an EKG machine.

When the nurse arrived, she attached electrodes to my chest as the doctor monitored my heart activity. My heart rate was far above the standard resting rate for a healthy 18 year-old, and he ordered some blood tests to be done. It would take a few days for those results to come back, so he offered little outside of a prescription for some flu medication.

The phrases "panic attack" or "anxiety disorder" never came up during this visit or visits to several other doctors in the weeks to follow. Likewise, I never really saw those conditions discussed when I searched for my symptoms online (the diagnosis for just about every symptom on medical message boards tended to be around the severity level of "super cancer"). It seems like there are tons of resources for sufferers of anxiety now, so I'm not sure if I wasn't looking in the right places or if psychological disorders were less of a part of the national conversation in 2003. Looking back, it wouldn't surprise me if this were the case in the 50s or 60s, but

I'm still surprised that I wasn't able to find much of any information about anxiety as recently as the 2000s.

With another scary experience under my belt and no real answers to speak of, I continued my new routine of laying in bed all day while hoping to feel better. My winter break was about to end, which I dreaded considering that my symptoms had only worsened since New Year's Day. Feeling like hell, I left the comfort of my childhood home and headed back to the hectic world of the dorms with some flu medication and a whole new suite of situations that I could fear attacks in.

My blood test results came in, and to my surprise they said that everything was completely normal. Nothing in the results hinted at anything out of the ordinary, which would have been a relief in any other situation but only added to the mystery here. I wanted to hear that some particular part of my body was wildly malfunctioning, and that I'd be as good as new after getting on a specific medication or having some procedure done. Instead, I was back to lying in bed with a 102-degree fever while my mind tried to wrap itself around what the hell was wrong with me.

This cycle continued into February with no signs of improvement. At this point, I had felt deathly ill and mentally exhausted for over three weeks. If I wasn't fighting to keep my breathing and heart rate under control, I was dizzy from a high fever. In the times that I was actually able to fall asleep, I'd wake up in the middle of the night, disoriented, sweating, and unable to fall back asleep. Laying in bed hadn't helped anything, so I told myself that getting up and being active would help shake me out of this funk. I asked my friends if they wanted to go see *Adaptation*, and part of me wondered if these attacks were somehow spurred on by seeing movies in theaters. This all sounds insane now, but I was grasping at straws for any kind of explanation. The initial attack happened at a movie, and the follow-up was during another movie, so that's about as much of a connection as I had seen up to that point. If it happened a third time, then I could be fairly confident that something about the theater environment was triggering these attacks.

Instead of being polite enough to wait until the end of the movie, my symptoms decided they'd show up early and stick around for the duration. I tried to stick it out for over an hour, but eventually fell into the same fate of the previous two theater visits. There I was in the bathroom, head in hands and wondering what the hell a movie theater could be doing to my body. I still had no idea how to lessen these symptoms, and all I had was some DayQuil in my pocket. I broke the capsules out of their pouch and distinctly remember my hand shaking like the world's lamest junkie as I tried to bring the cold medicine to my mouth near the bathroom's water fountain.

That weekend, I drove back to my mom's house and stayed there, away from the hectic campus and dorm life. I saw two different doctors, neither of which offered any answers. On one late night, I went to the emergency room, convinced that my heart was near some kind of fatal condition. After a series of tests and talks with the doctor, my mother and I were informed that there was absolutely nothing physically wrong with me.

My mother knew that I had been complaining about being sick, but thought something was odd about my behavior. On the way home from the emergency room, I remember her earnestly asking me if I was on drugs. All I could do was say no, as I still wasn't anywhere near comfortable with discussing the truth of the matter with her or anyone else.

Diagnosis

When I went back to school the next week, I decided that I'd give the campus medical facility a shot. I expected the same song and dance about how it was probably just the flu, but the doctor's immediate response shocked me.

"It sounds like you're describing a panic attack," he said.

I had probably heard that phrase in some context at some point in my life, but I had no sense of what it meant and certainly hadn't thought of it in conjunction with my current situation. He explained it to me, and asked me what I was doing whenever I felt them coming on suddenly.

"I was in movie theaters during the three biggest ones," I said. "So that doesn't make sense. I love movies, and I've seen tons of them in the theaters without any problems at all until recently."

He asked me if I was undergoing any major life changes that had brought about added day-to-day stress, and I told him that yes, I had been stressed for months thanks to the transition to college life. The doctor explained to me that the initial panic attack was probably a watershed moment for all of that pent-up anxiety, and that the subsequent theater attacks happened because I was unconsciously reminded of the circumstances surrounding my first attack. It wasn't movies that I was suddenly deathly afraid of, it was panic attacks.

This was the very definition of panic disorder, he explained – the fear of more panic attacks. They're so traumatic that the sufferer is terrified of experiencing more of them, and begins to avoid situations that may produce them.

I was floored. It was a totally new concept to me, but it was the first thing anyone had said that sounded like it made any sense at all. Why else would I feel like I was on the verge of death, despite nothing being physically wrong with me? I explained to the doctor that the physical sensations I had felt were very real...I wasn't imagining the heavy breathing, the rapid heartbeats, the sweating, etc. He immediately explained that the sensations were indeed real, but it was nothing more than my body activating "fight or flight" at inappropriate times.

The way he said all of this in such a matter-of-fact way made me feel so much better. It meant that I wasn't some anomaly – this had to be somewhat common. I could find others that had experienced what I was going through, and I wouldn't have to feel as alone in this condition as I had for the past several weeks. MDs were usually quicker to prescribe medicine than recommend therapy in my experience, and he put me on a low dosage of Paxil and told me to come back in a month.

I left that office feeling better than I had at any point since New Year's Eve. A diagnosis meant that this was something that I could fix, right? Unfortunately, that moment of joy was short-lived. A diagnosis is a big step in the right direction, but it's far from a remedy for a chronic condition.

The doctor had told me that it would take a few weeks for the Paxil to take full effect, but my brain has always defaulted to optimism. After all, I knew what was going on now and I had medication that would specifically target the problem. Surely it'd only take a few days before I was back on my feet and laughing, playing video games with my new friends, and getting nervous about the right things (talking to girls) again.

To my surprise, it would take much more than optimism and a diagnosis to turn things around. My flu symptoms persisted for months, with frequent fevers occurring into the spring (actually, my ears would get hot and turn red every night for several years). I wasn't bedridden like I had been in those initial weeks, but I was quickly fatigued and never had the energy to do anything outside of occasionally going to class and playing some video games before bed. Even though the first semester of college had taught me that I love socializing and going to parties, I didn't go to any or have any alcohol for several months in this new semester.

To my disappointment, the Paxil prescription was not a magic pill that made all of these problems instantly disappear. Rather, it reminded me of the zombie-like feeling that I had experienced in elementary school after being prescribed Ritalin for ADHD. My fevers were still frequent, and now I had the added stress of worrying about what this medication was doing to me.

At this point in my life, I was writing, directing, and editing short films. Doing this was tremendously exciting for me, and I loved showing them to friends, taking my projects around to film festivals, and submitting them for awards. I worried that the Paxil would drain me of whatever creative energy I had, and I was becoming increasingly concerned about the fact that it wasn't actually helping to alleviate any of my symptoms. The last straw came when I made the (always poor) decision to read the reactions that other people had to the medication. I read numerous horror stories on message boards in which Paxil users described how the drug had "ruined their life" or intensified their symptoms, and I stopped taking it immediately. In hindsight, this was likely a poor decision. It can take many weeks for a new medication to fully take effect, and I hadn't even given it a real chance before I dropped it. Paxil's initial negative effects turned me off immediately, however, and I might have given up too quickly as a result.

The euphoria I felt when leaving the doctor's office upon my diagnosis had mostly faded. Sure, I had more answers than before, but that knowledge wasn't exactly making the symptoms any easier to deal with. And now, the magic pill that was supposed to laser in on my condition had turned out to be a dud. I want to note that it may have been ineffective for me, but this might not be the case for others with anxiety. I'll talk about this later, but different people have wildly different reactions to medication. For someone else, Paxil may have tremendously positive effects. It wasn't the answer for me, however.

When I decided to stop taking Paxil, I may have turned too harshly in the wrong direction. I still don't think medication is the magic key to solving anxiety issues (spoiler: that magic key doesn't exist), but I went so far in the opposite way that I swore off *any* medication for many years. I wouldn't take any cold medication when I was sick. I wouldn't get flu shots. In the most extreme case I can think of, I refused to take any pain medication when I had a molar taken out or when I had all four wisdom teeth removed. Like an idiot, I sat around for the entire wisdom teeth recovery process without taking the highly effective pain medication that I had been prescribed. I was so worried about feeling zombified or "high" that I put myself through a lot of unnecessary pain, and I've become less stubborn about that in recent years.

I wasn't quite back at square one, but I was back in the scary position of feeling terrible on a daily basis and still not knowing what to do about it. The doctor told me to come back in a month, but I assumed he'd just prescribe me a different medication, so I never followed up with him. Part of me hoped that the Paxil itself was what was causing my feelings of anxiety during the time I was on it. When I went off of it, I was discouraged by another night of panic attacks letting me know that this would be a longer battle than I had hoped.

Doctors didn't seem to know a solid solution to my issues, and I felt uncomfortable talking to my mother about it since she probably still thought that I was on drugs. Despite having a great relationship with my father, I knew this wasn't the kind of thing he'd be sympathetic towards. I didn't have anyone that I felt comfortable talking to about my anxiety, so I wrote in a journal for a brief period of time. I found this journal in storage recently, and an entry from the end of February 2003 illustrates my mindset at the time:

Been doing a lot of thinking about my medical situation lately. I had another bad experience, which lets me know that this might not be going away as quickly as I might have hoped.

It's clear now that I have a serious problem concerning my throat, and an even more serious problem regarding the mental state I've lapsed into about once or twice a day (the "drugged" feeling).

I wish I could convey better to Mom (and the rest of the family) just what the "bad spells" are like. I don't think she has any idea how horrible they really are. She thinks (rightfully so) that it's all in my head. I wish she could know the sheer dread that these attacks cause. Choking, trouble breathing, stomachaches, fever, chills, and an overwhelming sense that I might be losing my mind. The five or six of these attacks in the last week-and-a-half have easily been the most terrifying experiences of my life. Mom is tired of hearing about it, and I can't say I blame her. It's all I've talked about for over fifty days now.

It's been difficult, but I'm confident that I will come out of this situation a better and stronger person. This situation can be seen as opportunity just as much as it can be seen as an affliction.

At the time of that entry, it seemed that I was still partially hoping for a biological explanation for the attacks. I made mention of serious problems with my throat, which in hindsight is just referring to one of the many symptoms I experience whenever my anxiety spikes. Having trouble swallowing food and feeling like there's a lump in my throat have been two of the longest-running sensations that my anxiety disorders have caused.

That journal entry also touches on something extremely important for anxiety sufferers and those that may be close to them. Panic attacks and generalized anxiety are *very* difficult to explain to the portion of the population that has never struggled with these conditions. It's easy for many people to equate panic attacks to sometime in the past in which they got nervous while giving a speech or performing in a play, but anxiety disorders are much different. Situational examples like a speech or a play can make anyone nervous, not just those with chronic anxiety. One of the hardest things to deal with when dealing with anxiety disorders is when these attacks happen when there's no real reason for them. My first attacks weren't while I was giving speeches or getting ready to jump out of a plane. They happened while I was seeing movies, which has always been one of my favorite activities. I've had them while I've been playing video games by myself, spending a nice afternoon in with a girlfriend, or going on a jog. Panic attacks are often triggered by seemingly nothing, which is one of the most frustrating and confusing aspects of these disorders.

If you're a relative or a friend of someone that tells you that they're struggling with feelings like these, you need to believe them. There's nothing to be gained by making these symptoms up, so that son/daughter/brother/sister/friend is likely struggling with something very real and just needs someone to talk to. I don't fault my parents for the way they reacted to my first complaints about these symptoms. They didn't have any knowledge of what anxiety disorders were, and they gradually became more understanding and accepting of the condition as the years went on and they learned more about it. I hope that more and more people have at least some knowledge of anxiety disorders as the years go on and mental illness is more widely discussed. For those of us that struggle with them on a daily basis, few things are as helpful as having close friends or relatives that are willing to lend an ear and try to understand what you're going through, regardless of whether they've experienced similar feelings themselves.

When I look at old journal entries from this period, I'm glad to see that I remained optimistic even in this confusing and terrifying period of my life. In the middle of some of these attack-filled nights, I distinctly remember having the thought of "If I make it to the end of 2003 without being in a padded cell, it'll be a miracle." It's easy to fear that an attack will never end while you're in the middle of one. The brain starts coming up with every worst case scenario that it can, but then there inevitably comes a point where it just...ends. It seems like the brain reaches some kind of threshold for anxiety that it can't support for long periods of time, and every panic attack reaches an end. Years later, I'd adopt "It always ends" as a kind of mantra whenever I caught myself in the middle of an attack. They're so terrible at the time and they seem like they'll never end, but there always comes a peak, and it always ends. Reminding myself of that is one of the most important tactics I've taught myself to think of whenever I'm in the middle of an attack, but it took many more years of struggling before I learned that particular lesson.

The Importance of Opening Up

In those first six months of dealing with panic disorder, I was constantly waiting for the magic solution that would "fix" me for good. I wanted a biological explanation that could be fixed with a simple procedure. I wanted to find a pill that would permanently level out whatever chemicals in my brain were misbalanced. Maybe I just had a really bad flu that came with some odd psychological side effects.

Six months in, I was starting to realize that this was not going to be an easy fix. Most of my flu symptoms disappeared after the first few months, but I still had the odd sensation of my ears getting red and hot every night like clockwork. Medication was something that I wanted no part of after the Paxil experiment, and I wouldn't consider it again for many years. It was time for me to find new ways of dealing with this problem, but I didn't quite know where to start.

Despite being fairly directionless at this point, I still took solace in the fact that I had a diagnosis. My enemy had a name now, and I knew how to find others that were going through the same thing I was. It would be years before I started talking openly about these problems with family and friends, so I found comfort in the anonymous nature of the internet. I no longer had to type a bunch of symptoms into WebMD and be terrified at the myriad results filled with awful-sounding diseases. All I had to do was type "panic disorder message board" into Google and was instantly directed to several active communities of users with anxiety.

Nights were always the worst, as I'd lay in bed with a racing mind that would inevitably start fixating on my condition. These were the times that I'd force myself to get up and look at threads on the message boards, reminding myself that I wasn't alone. I'd scroll through thread after thread, nodding as I recognized so many stories that mirrored my own. I'd feel more comfortable, and eventually my mind would settle down or exhaust itself and I'd be able to sleep (even if it happened to be 6am before this happened).

After many months of using message boards as my primary form of communication regarding anxiety, I decided to take the next step. Knowing that psychologists were simply for therapy and couldn't prescribe medication, I felt more comfortable going to one since I knew they wouldn't just scribble a prescription down and send me on my way. I saw several campus psychologists at the University of Kansas, and while I don't remember them saying anything particularly profound, it helped to talk face-to-face and at length to someone with knowledge of these matters.

One of them pointed me towards an anxiety support group that was held weekly on campus. Speaking in front of crowds was something that always triggered anxiety for me, but I assumed that this particular scenario would be easier considering that I'd be among others that would understand. I only went to a handful of these meetings, but they were certainly eye-opening. As I waited my turn to speak, I listened to story after story that let me know that I might not be as far gone as I thought I was. Living in my own little anxiety bubble, it was easy to think that I was the only one that had it this bad and that no one would ever understand how awful it got. Listening to the others that spoke before me, I realized that not only did they have it as bad as me, but many had it noticeably worse. I distinctly remember one girl that couldn't even look up as she spoke. She stared down at her fidgeting hands and softly told her story, stumbling over her words repeatedly. I was struggling for sure, but as I watched her I realized how much worse things could be. She described not being able to leave the house, and that she had spent the entire previous night tossing and turning in bed out of fear of talking in front of this support group. I certainly felt my heart rate rise and I started to get nervous as my turn approached, but it was nowhere near the struggle this girl was going through.

The point of that last paragraph wasn't me thinking "Whew, at least I'm not like her!". I felt awful for her, as I couldn't even imagine how rough she had it on a day-to-day basis. I didn't feel relief that I wasn't as far down the anxiety rabbit hole as her, I simply gained perspective. All it took was that one girl to struggle through her story to make me realize that I didn't live in some awful little bubble that no one could understand. She understood more than I did, and yet here she was telling her story no matter how difficult it was for her. Fighting through intense anxiety in an effort to improve your condition is another key skill to learn, but it's another one that I wouldn't fully understand and utilize for years.

Telling my (relatively tame by comparison) story stirred up some jitters and fidgeting, but I got through it. It was once I was outside of the company of fellow anxiety sufferers that I really struggled with drawing any attention to myself. This feeling existed before my first panic attacks, even. During high school, I dreaded the idea of walking into class late. Even if it was just a minute or two after the bell rang, I couldn't bring myself to enter the classroom out of fear of everyone turning and looking at me. If I was driving to school and running late in the morning, I'd park in a nearby neighborhood and sit in my car for the entire duration of the first class. Once the bell rang again at 8:50am to signify the end of 1st hour, I'd walk into the school and go to my 2nd hour class on time. It's for the same reason that I always preferred to be behind the camera while I was making my short films. I loved writing, editing, and directing, but I never wanted to draw any actual attention to myself back then (this probably sounds absurd to anyone who follows me in my current line of work).

Once I had experienced full-blown panic attacks, this feeling only intensified. I'd sit in large college lecture halls as they did roll call, and feel my breathing speed up as they got closer to the R names. I'd try to slow my breathing, thinking "In just a minute or two, I'll say 'here' and this will all be over." I wasn't required to say anything beyond that one word, and no one would have even turned their head to look at me when I did. I knew this, but it still spiked my anxiety every single time. On some occasions, I remember my hands and feet going numb and my vision becoming black around the edges as the calling of my name approached.

These new fears started carrying over into my work life, as well. At the time, I raised money for the University of Kansas by working in a call center that secured donations from alumni. Each semester, the entire room of 24 callers would take turns standing up and introducing themselves to any new hires that came on board. This would typically go on for about two weeks at the beginning of each semester, and each day would involve us telling a different "fun fact" about ourselves. All I would have had to do is stand up for about 10 seconds, say my name, year in school, hometown, and my favorite movie/song/candy/whatever. Like with the roll call situation, I'd feel the symptoms intensify every time it got closer to my turn. If the person right before me was taking longer than usual to tell a story or fact about themselves, the panic would increase exponentially until I wondered if I might pass out.

I knew I couldn't maintain these daily spikes in anxiety on a regular basis, so I went to a campus psychologist again. He suggested that I be open about my condition and explain my difficulties to my boss, and that most employers would respect that and do whatever they can to help. For my classes, he pointed me towards my school's Students with Disabilities department (which I had no previous knowledge of). The idea of opening up about my anxiety to school officials and my boss intimidated me, but it was less scary than the idea of continuing to dread these daily occurrences.

I went to my boss at the call center that night and asked if she had a moment. We had never talked about anything serious before and didn't really know each other well personally, so I instantly felt awkward as I started explaining the situation to her. I made a point of being completely open about it and explaining my situation, but I wanted to make sure that she wouldn't stop doing something the rest of the staff enjoyed (the introductions) on account of me. Her response was reassuring, letting me know that she had family members with similar problems and that she wanted to do whatever she could to help. She let me know that I could come into work 30 minutes late each day, which would get me there just in time to skip the intros and get started on actual work. Once the two-week introduction period was over, we'd get right back to a normal schedule. I was really surprised at how natural and helpful that conversation was, and it's something that has stuck with me for years.

From that moment on, I made a point to explain my anxiety situation to any new bosses at every job I had. That way, they'd know what was going on if I had to step outside for a moment to get a breather or something along those lines. Just knowing that my bosses were aware of my condition did wonders towards putting me at ease on a day to day basis. In all of these years of explaining my anxiety to employers, not one has responded in a negative way.

Whether they knew anything about anxiety disorders or not, each and every one of them listened to what I had to say and responded in a way that made me feel better. This was one of my earliest experiences that taught me that being open about mental disorders is an incredibly important and helpful way to feel more comfortable in personal and professional situations.

Next up was the Students with Disabilities department. I didn't feel as uncomfortable with this meeting, as they were surely experienced in situations like mine. As I suspected, they had a plan ready to go for me. I was handed a sheet of paper with a list of requests, allowing me to check boxes for additional time on exams, a private testing room, optional attendance, personal study appointments with teachers, and plenty more. I didn't want to take too much advantage of the situation by just checking everything, so I made sure that attendance was my key focus so that I wouldn't have to participate in roll call. That way, I could walk into class a few minutes later, avoiding the anxiety and still taking in the material of the day.

Later, I did find it easy to go against my initial vow to not take advantage of the situation. While everything I said to the office was factual, it was tempting to skip class on a regular basis since I knew that it would never count against my grade. I skipped classes entirely, sometimes for months at a time as I opted to spend my time reviewing video games for a local newspaper. This is one of the only things that I've done in my quest to conquer anxiety that I'm not particularly proud of. I took advantage of a piece of paper that said I didn't have to go to class, even in classes that didn't do roll calls or require me to speak in front of people. Things worked out for me in the end, but I wouldn't recommend stepping outside of the bounds of what's necessary for anyone else that asks for help from a similar department at their school.

Two of my biggest stressors were now non-factors, which allowed me to breathe more easily. There was one other major worry for me, and that was the required presentations in the classes I was enrolled in. In the past, I had dropped these courses entirely when I saw a presentation on the syllabus. Other classes were required for me to graduate, however, and I'd have to figure out another way to get through these. Considering that my discussions with my call center boss and Students with Disabilities had gone so smoothly, I decided to be open about things and contact my teachers directly. I still have the email account that I used back then, so I found the following email exchange with one of my film teachers:

From me to the teacher:

Hi [Teacher],

Just got back from class, and I'm slightly concerned about it. The reason I say this is because I've developed a pretty intense panic disorder over the last year/year and a half. I'm currently seeing a medical doctor and a psychologist about it, and I'm trying to get it figured out.

It doesn't make much sense to me, as I'm not a shy person by any means. However, for some reason, I've had countless full-scale panic attacks in very minor situations. To give you an idea of how bad it is, I'm always on the verge of a panic attack even when I have to say "here" during class roll calls. I almost had three just in the class with you today - once when you called on me because you thought my hand was raised, once when I had to read the dichotomy card (I almost couldn't even say the words), and another time when you looked at me to ask about the "gregarious" thing. I've had to drop several classes for this very reason (as soon as I see a presentation on the syllabus, I drop).

Lately, it seems like I can only function in classes where I'm just in the back of the class, virtually invisible. I can't even handle roll calls, let alone standing in front of a camera or standing up to do a spot check of my journal.

I'm not sure what exactly to do, because I need to graduate soon, and you recommended this class to me as something I should take to make that happen sooner. Would it be possible to do something on my own accord to get the credit for the class? I'd be fine with putting together projects on my own, I just can't do anything that would require me to be in front of a camera or in front of the class in any way.

Obviously, I can provide a doctor's note to validate this

if you'd like. I have an appointment coming up soon, so it shouldn't be a problem by any means.

Any help would be greatly appreciated.

Sincerely,
Dan Ryckert

His response:

Wow. I am sorry to hear about that, My son and wife have panic attacks and agoraphobia/claustrophobia that they deal with medically, so I am familiar with your predicament. Are you on any medications? There are several good ones out there.

I don't think there will be a problem with having you participate in the class without having to do presentations. I'm not sure if you want to let anyone else know about your condition, and will respect your decision either way.

Perhaps you can present your ideas to the class via email, or in a chat format. You could also screen projects w/o being present, and just get written responses. (This doesn't affect your production ability, does it?)

Anyway, let's see what we can do to work around this.

-[Teacher]

Sure enough, he responded with just as much understanding as everyone else that I had actually opened up to about it. Feeling better and better, I sent another teacher a similar email and quickly received the following response:

Hi Dan,

I sympathize with your situation. Thanks for being so forthright. I'll be in my office on Monday morning working on grades. Please see me or contact me and we'll work out something. Don't worry about your grade, okay? I promise you we'll work it out. I hope I didn't seem impatient in class the other night. It's just that so many students at the last minute come up with all sorts of problems...But I know you are sincere. So don't worry, okay?

My cell phone is (X). And my office phone is (X). Call me Monday.

[Teacher]

At this point, I was starting to realize that opening up about my anxiety disorders wasn't the terrifying concept that I once thought it to be. Every single person in the academic or professional world that I opened up to about this responded in the most helpful ways possible, which immediately eliminated major, daily triggers for me. Part of me wonders if it's because firing a person or failing them out of a class because of a medical condition might have legal repercussions, but I prefer to believe that these were just sympathetic people that wanted to help someone that was struggling. Opening up to people in my personal life was still a scary idea, but getting work and school taken care of was tremendously reassuring and a massive step in the right direction for me.

DAN RYCKERT

Trial and Error

A couple of years into my experience with anxiety disorders, I had already overcome two of the toughest initial barriers. One was accepting that this would be a long fight with no magic solution. The other was discovering the importance of opening up about what I was going through. While these are huge steps that anyone struggling with anxiety eventually needs to go through, I had a long ways to go before I could finally see the light at the end of the tunnel.

Both of those steps are important, but they aren't necessarily things that will alleviate the actual symptoms. Now that I was more comfortable with what panic disorder entailed, it was time to figure out how to make things better. I spent more time on mental health message boards and began reading any book I could find on the subject. As is the case with just about any medical condition, opinions varied wildly about the best remedies.

One common thread that kept coming up was the benefit of physical exercise. At no point in my life had I been particularly athletic, and I had never exercised on a regular basis outside of a high school weights class that I barely participated in. With that class being my only real experience with exercise, I started going to the campus gym without any idea of what the hell I was doing. I'd sit down at various weight machines, guess an amount to lift, and go through a few motions with horrible form until I didn't want to do it any more (which didn't take long, typically). I had no disciplined workout regimen, and as such I was destined to fail. Little weight was lost, little muscle was gained, and little progress was made in terms of my anxiety in the few months that I half-heartedly went to the gym.

That "magic pill" that I wanted early on in my disorder didn't exist, but I hadn't given up on the idea of something helping me out in some way. My experience with Paxil had soured me on prescription medication, so I went to an organic food store that offered an assortment of herbal remedies. Many users of mental health message boards recommended St. John's Wort, so I picked up a bottle and took it daily for a few months. There was no noticeable benefit that I was experiencing with this new supplement, so I dropped it once the bottle was empty.

Most of what I was trying during this period wasn't working, and much of it was due to my inability to commit. As I'll discuss later, exercise wound up being one of the most effective ways to combat anxiety, but my heart wasn't in it at this stage. I have no doubt that I would have gotten a head start on easing my anxiety if I had done some basic research on exercise and found a particular approach to it that worked for me, but I was grasping at straws during these years and was too quick to ditch certain approaches without doing the right research.

It was during this period (roughly 2005-2007) that I started experiencing some additional and certainly unwanted symptoms. I briefly dated a girl at this time, and I remember going to Applebee's with her once. As I ate, I started worrying about my throat not being able to swallow properly. Odd sensations in my esophagus had been a common experience ever since the early days of my anxiety problems, but it had never really given me problems while eating. On this occasion, I tried to swallow a bite of pasta but quickly coughed it up to my embarrassment. My mind had been worrying so much about swallowing that I actually started having trouble doing it, and I had to explain why it happened to the girl I was dating (becoming one of the first people outside of doctors, work, or school that I did this with).

From that day, I had trouble swallowing food for years. In college, I'd imagine I was one of the few "adults" who bought chewable multivitamins because I worried about getting the full Centrum tabs down my throat. I still struggle with swallowing to this day, mostly when I'm at a restaurant and eating with a group of people. Anyone who's eaten out with me has surely noticed how I almost always leave about half of my meal uneaten, and I take the rest home in a box. It's never because I don't like the food or I'm not hungry, it's just that I struggle with swallowing in these situations. If I went out to eat with co-workers for lunch, I'd almost always bring at least half of my meal back and finish it at my desk so that they wouldn't have to sit and watch me slowly eat for another half hour. It's an annoying thing for me personally, but I'll take it over full-blown panic attacks at a restaurant any day of the week.

I picked up another habit during this time that still hasn't completely gone away. After years of having terrible vision, I had LASIK surgery so that I'd be free of glasses and contacts (at least temporarily...my vision would continue to degrade in later years). As anyone who's had the surgery can attest, your eyes feel very dry for weeks after the procedure. It's not dissimilar to the feeling of wearing contacts and having them dry out substantially. My way of combating this feeling was to close my eyes and roll them around briefly, which helped alleviate the dry feeling. For whatever reason (and I suspect this may be a bit of my OCD peeking through), I continued to do this involuntarily long after the side effects of the surgery had ceased. It's something I'm aware of and have tried to stop for almost ten years, but it's one of the more stubborn habits to come out of all of this. Watch any of my on-camera appearances I did back when I was at Game Informer, and you're sure to notice it at least a few times. It's very apparent during a panel I did for Giant Bomb in 2014, which is an event that I'll discuss in detail later.

These habits started around this time and have survived longer than I'd like, but they're both extremely minor compared to the sheer dread I was experiencing years before this. A more substantial struggle that reared its head around this time was the realization that panic disorder was not the only anxiety-related condition that I had.

Panic disorder is largely situational. Most of the time, it involves panic attacks that occur in predictable circumstances like public speaking, driving in heavy traffic, or being in the middle of packed crowds. These attacks also tend to be short-lived, rarely lasting longer than 20 minutes or so. What concerned me was that I started having longer feelings of unexplainable anxiety in situations that absolutely did not call for it. I'd be sitting on my couch watching TV or working on a video game review in my pajama pants (far from anxiety-provoking situations), and suddenly feel a wave of dread wash over me. It would get to the point where I couldn't do anything at all, even things as simple as paying attention to a TV show or movie. I was familiar with the uncomfortable feelings that anxiety brings about, but this was particularly confusing to me considering that I couldn't think of a single reason why it would be happening at these times.

Unlike my onset of panic disorder, I actually had some direction when it came to resources this time around. After asking around on mental health message boards about these symptoms, they suggested that I might also have generalized anxiety disorder. Never one to take internet comments as gospel (a bad idea no matter what topic you're looking up, generally), I went to the campus psychologist again. As I expected, he gave me the official diagnosis.

Learning that I had generalized anxiety disorder wasn't a massive blow on the level of my onset of panic disorder, but it certainly didn't help. Before, my anxiety was largely predictable. I knew it wasn't going to be fun if I had to sit through a roll call situation, but at least I knew what was going to happen. With GAD, that looming specter of anxiety could appear at literally any time. I started experiencing prolonged anxiety during times that I was playing video games, spending time with my family, driving to work, laying in bed, or any other typically benign situation. The symptoms weren't new, but their ability to pop up on a whim certainly was.

It was around this time that I decided to talk to my mother more about my issues. Considering that it had now been years of me occasionally bringing it up, she seemed to be beginning to understand that this wasn't just a temporary thing or me being on drugs. She told me that she had spoken to a neighbor about what I was describing, and he swore up and down that hypnotherapy helped him out. I realize that the placebo effect can have a very real impact, but I always preferred to do some research before I jumped into anything. I did some quick searches and came away skeptical of hypnotherapy's legitimacy, so I let her know that I appreciated the suggestion but wasn't interested in pursuing it. She asked around a bit at work and learned that her boss had a history with severe anxiety.

She let me know that he was willing to chat with me about what's worked for him, and I jumped at the chance. The only people I had talked to that knew anything about anxiety were psychologists and family members of those with the condition, but no one that had firsthand experience of their own (outside of hearing brief stories from that support group). I reached out to him via email, and he didn't take long to respond with his history of struggling with the condition. Having this line of communication open up made me feel great, and I looked forward to having a long conversation with someone that could relate to what I had been going through for the past few years.

My hopes got shot down with the next email. He wasted no time when it came to suggesting a spiritual solution, explaining that my anxiety came as a result of having a hole in my soul thanks to not having a "personal relationship with Christ." I'm completely fine with people taking whatever approach works for them, but I knew that suddenly becoming a religious convert wasn't the solution for me. We continued to talk for a while after I explained that I wasn't religious, but it became clear that every road kept leading straight to Jesus for him. It never got contentious, but I ended the conversation thread and decided to continue looking for other avenues.

I wanted to talk openly about my anxiety with those close to me, so I decided that it was time to try to talk to my dad about it for the first time. Unfortunately, his reaction was exactly what I expected. I've always had an amazing relationship with my father, but his personality isn't one that would take the time to learn about or understand something like anxiety disorders. Not long into me trying to explain the situation, he started saying things like "Just chill out, what's the problem?" and "What do you have to worry about? You're fine."

Reacting like this certainly isn't a sign of him being some uncaring, cold father, as it's an extremely common occurrence when family members are first told about anxiety concerns. For those that don't have any knowledge about conditions like these, it's confusing to hear people describe feeling intense dread when there are no pressing concerns. I was disappointed by the reaction, but not surprised. Thankfully, he'd very slowly come around in terms of being sympathetic about it, likely helped in no small part years later by his daughter experiencing identical symptoms at the exact same age mine started.

My dad was unhelpful, and the only other person with anxiety that I had met wanted me to spend my time praying that my symptoms would just disappear. I needed someone else to talk to, and I'd find it in someone I should have contacted right at the beginning.

A Summer of Improvement

I needed a new plan for fighting my symptoms. It was obvious that I didn't yet have the right commitment to exercise, and my brief attempts at it were never enough to see the great benefits it can provide. As I read message boards in search for a new approach, I noticed many people mentioning the effectiveness of meditation. My only experience with meditation was that brief ten minutes in Buddy's psychology class from six months before my first panic attack. For some reason, the idea of exploring meditation further never came to my mind during my (at this point) years-long struggle with anxiety.

My school listed its faculty online, as well as their email addresses. I wasn't sure if Buddy still taught at the school, as we hadn't kept in touch once I finished that summer program. His name popped up when I searched, so I sent him an email describing my situation. I explained that the ten minutes of meditation years ago left me with a sense of calm that I appreciated even before I struggled with daily anxiety, and I was curious if he knew anything about its applications towards chronic anxiety.

He gave me the answer I was hoping for. As I should have expected, meditation was especially effective for those that suffer from a variety of anxiety disorders. This was a lesson that I learned time and time again for years as I talked to experts, friends with anxiety, and visited message boards. Plus, it didn't sound like that crazy of a commitment to make. Buddy mentioned in that class that our lives would change with an hour of meditation each day, but even ten minutes produced a very noticeable calming effect.

In addition to my email conversation with Buddy, I started regularly reading about meditation in books and on the internet. It didn't take long to realize that there are a ton of different approaches and schools of thought when it comes to meditation, and I wanted to find one that focused on the psychological benefits and eschewed anything that pushed too far in the spiritual direction. This took a lot of trial and error, including going to some classes that seemed straightforward at the outset but quickly ventured into new age mystical territory that I didn't subscribe to. I wasn't trying to unlock the secrets of the universe or hear about chakras…I just wanted to not be so damn nervous all the time.

At some point during my weeks of researching this, I was hanging out with a friend from the call center job. We were having some beers at her place, and when I went to the bathroom I noticed that she had a note on her mirror that had one word on it: "Mindfulness." I walked back to the living room and asked her what that was all about, and she mentioned that she put it there as a reminder to do mindfulness meditation every day.

I had probably seen mindfulness mentioned during my searches, but for some reason I never really went link diving on that particular approach. As she explained it to me, it sounded exactly like what I was looking for. That weekend, I checked out a book on the subject and made sure to specifically search for mindfulness when I was looking for meditation info on the internet.

There are a *lot* of books out there that dive into the nitty-gritty of what mindfulness is in a manner that's far more educated than me, so I won't spend too much time attempting to break down the science. Here's the very short version: mindfulness is essentially the act of putting some time aside to intentionally take in and recognize the present moment. It's about focus on the breath and the sensations that are currently happening in your body, without letting your brain be filled with thoughts or worries about the past or future. When a thought like "Oh, I need to get groceries tonight" or "I hope I didn't say the wrong thing at work today" enters your mind, you're supposed to acknowledge and accept that the thought appeared, but let it float away without spending any additional time dwelling on it or following that train of thought.

Again, that's about as basic as it gets, and that's because there are other books, classes, and websites that do a deep dive on the learning process and different techniques. Some people focus on sounds that are happening around them, others count in their heads for a specific length of time for each in breath and out breath, and others prefer to not focus on any one thing in particular. Some prefer to practice mindfulness in the traditional cross-legged seated position, while others do it laying down in bed before sleep. Another form is called walking meditation, and it involves walking very slowly while being mindful of every single step and the sensations that arise in the body.

My method in these early days of practice (and for most of my future years) was simple. Once a day, I'd sit down cross-legged in a quiet room and set my phone's timer for ten minutes. After hitting start, I'd immediately try to focus solely on the present while avoiding the torrent of thoughts and worries that would typically invade my consciousness. Something that I learned early on (and you will too if you try it) is that I was *terrible* at this. My brain immediately went into autopilot, and within 30 seconds I usually had three or four different threads of thought bouncing around while I was trying to do the exact opposite.

Many people feel discouraged when they experience this early in a meditation practice, but the key thing to remember is that it's just that – a practice. You're not going to start draining three-pointers the first time you pick up a basketball, and you're not going to have extended meditation sessions free from unwanted thoughts right when you decide to try mindfulness. I'd frequently get restless as I waited for the alarm to signal that the ten minutes were up, and open my eyes to see six minutes still remaining on the clock.

I can't stress enough that this is not an easy process when you start, but these difficult first experiences can really teach you a lot about your own brain. When I was just going about my usual days before I started practicing meditation, these same thoughts were rattling around inside my head during every waking hour. It was once I tried to sit down and focus on the present that I actually realized this. "Holy crap, this is what my brain is automatically doing *all day???*" was a frequent thought after these sessions. It's no surprise that anxiety comes about when the brain's default state is one of constant thoughts and worries about the past and future.

It didn't take long for my meditation practice to start having a very real effect on my day-to-day life and decision-making. Before I started my practice, I was wandering through life on autopilot without putting much actual thought into what I was doing. Sure, I'd be able to go through all the motions of getting up on time, going to work, socializing, and plenty more without much issue, but my mind was frequently elsewhere. Being more mindful in day-to-day life can make an immediate impact on little things you'd never expect.

A common exercise when someone is learning mindfulness involves eating a single cashew (although this can be done to similar effect with a raisin, a cracker, etc). When presented with a bowl full of cashews, many people will mindlessly shove several of them in their mouth at a time, over and over, without really processing what the taste of a single one of them is like. This exercise tasks people with dedicating a good amount of time to thinking about one cashew before ever taking a bite. You start by holding it in the palm of your hand, feeling the weight as you roll it around. Then you pinch it between your fingers and feel the texture and contours of the cashew. Next, you raise it to your nose and smell it before finally putting it into your mouth. Even then, you don't bite just yet. You roll it around in your mouth for several seconds as you taste the exterior of the cashew. Then, you bite into it and focus on the taste as you chew before swallowing.

This exercise isn't meant to represent the way you should eat from now on, as it's simply meant as an illustration of how much a sensation can be amplified and improved if you really take the time to focus on it. When I did this exercise for the first time, I remember thinking it was silly that I was taking so much time preparing to eat just one cashew. When I bit into it, I realized that all that time spent thinking about and focusing on it had seriously affected my appreciation of its flavor. I'd typically go through a whole tin of cashews while watching TV or occupying my mind with something else, and that would never even give me the chance to focus on and savor the taste. Eating one cashew with mindfulness was more rewarding than eating an entire tin mindlessly.

This realization got me thinking about how mindfulness could affect other elements of my life. An immediate application was in the way I ate. I had long been a regular customer of just about every fast food chain you can name, but I realized that I could probably get more enjoyment out of eating healthy food mindfully than by cramming a bunch of fries or potato chips into my mouth without even thinking about them.

It was the right time for this revelation, as I was at the most physically unhealthy I had ever been. Forget the "freshman 15," as I had spent the first few years of college going from 155 pounds to 196. It certainly wasn't muscle, as I never exercised and was quickly growing a beer gut thanks to my now-frequent partying. Once I decided to start being more mindful about decisions regarding my health, I made a promise to myself that I'd never hit 200 pounds (a promise that I've successfully kept to this day). I was still years away from learning smart ways to eat healthy, but I at least substantially cut down on the amount of junk food and fast food I was eating.

Mindfulness became a regular part of my day for weeks, and it kept resulting in me learning more things about my lifestyle and how it affected me. I started making graphs in Microsoft Excel that would give me a visual representation of my anxiety symptoms as they related to other activities. On one chart, I'd enter two numbers every day. One number was the intensity of my anxiety symptoms on a scale of 1-10. The other was how many alcoholic drinks I had drank on that date. After a couple of weeks, I noticed a clear correlation. Every day that I rated especially high on the anxiety scale was directly preceded by a night of heavy drinking. I plugged the numbers into a line chart, and there was no denying the direct correlation – I was dramatically more prone to panic attacks and general anxiety on days after I had been especially drunk.

This information came at a convenient time, as I had already been thinking about my use of alcohol before I had connected it with anxiety. In the years I had been in college, I had definitely fallen into a regular drinking schedule. It wasn't every night, but I'd always get significantly drunk on the 3-5 nights a week I'd go out. Despite not having a history of alcoholism in my family, I had already wanted to take an extended break from drinking just to ensure that I wasn't prone to substance addiction. The summer was about to arrive, and I decided that I'd go the entire three months without having a single sip of alcohol to see how the sobriety would affect my anxiety.

Not long after that, I decided to go one step further when it came to healthy decisions. With significantly more free time on my hands and access to a 24/7 fitness facility on campus, there was no better time to get serious about exercising. I had no idea what I was doing, but I started going to the gym every day and trying to find workouts that I enjoyed.

Since I never had a desire to "get big," weights didn't really appeal to me. I gravitated towards elliptical machines and treadmills, and eventually started timing my longer runs on an actual track. At one point, a friend recommended racquetball to me and we started playing daily. This was one of the first activities I found that gave me a great workout while I was genuinely enjoying what I was doing. I'd play for sixty minutes that felt like fifteen, then look at my heart rate monitor to learn that I had burned 600 calories while I was having a blast.

My summer went by exactly how I promised myself it would. I ran and played racquetball almost daily, and didn't have a single drop of alcohol. The experiment was a success on all fronts, which was made clear by me losing over thirty pounds and going back down to 165 for the first time in years.

Going from zero to 60 is not easy at all when it comes to beginning an exercise regimen. For most of my life, I assumed that I would hate all forms of working out. Those first couple of weeks at the gym brought back memories of hating weight class, as lifting weights never felt particularly rewarding to me. When I decided that running was probably a better avenue for me to explore, I was terrible at first. I was able to half-ass my way through a low-intensity elliptical workout, but couldn't get anywhere near a mile run on the treadmill or track without feeling like I was going to collapse.

It wasn't until I found ways to enjoy myself at the gym that I was able to really get into the groove of going every day. I bought my first iPod and loaded it with songs to make my now hour-long sessions on the elliptical more enjoyable. A stopwatch helped me log my lap and mile times on the track, which gave me quantifiable goals to shoot for that I could easily monitor progress of.

During these three months, I never once felt any kind of "I need a drink" sensation. This made me confident that alcoholism was a very unlikely trait for me, but I wanted to make sure that I was still being smart about booze. I love drinking and it was critical in terms of me "coming out of my shell" socially, but I had seen and heard enough stories of desperate alcoholics whose addiction started slow and then came on like a tidal wave. After the summer, I felt safe continuing to party and drink at the levels I did before, but I promised myself that I'd keep an eye on things and make the needed changes if anything ever started to get out of control. It's 2015 as I write this, and I've still never gotten into a fight, gotten into any real trouble with the law, or faced any serious negative consequences that have come out of my enjoyment of drinking (outside of some rough hangovers and an ever-changing level of beer gut).

I was confident that I wasn't an alcoholic, but before I started drinking again I promised myself that I'd never drink to relieve anxiety symptoms. That sounded like an easy way to slide into actual alcoholism, as I was some level of anxious every single day. Today, I'll occasionally have some drinks to feel more comfortable before doing something particularly stressful like appearing in front of an auditorium full of people, but I've never once drank to relieve symptoms as they've popped up.

Even after the three-month exercise/sobriety experiment, I continued updating two graphs so they'd serve as a constant reminder of what triggers my anxiety. One was the "Drinking vs. Anxiety" chart, and the other was an "Exercise vs. Anxiety" chart. The numbers made it clear – my anxiety spiked significantly during periods where I was drinking heavily, and decreased to low levels during periods where I was taking it easy on the booze and focusing on exercise. This has remained a constant for my entire life, and I can't imagine that things will ever change. So there's a revelation for you...regular exercise is better for your mental health than getting wasted several nights a week.

It took almost five years, but I was finally at a point in which I had learned enough about anxiety disorders and how to deal with them to make a major impact in my day-to-day well-being. Anxiety was still a daily occurrence, but major panic attacks were becoming rare and my periods of general anxiety were shorter and less intense. I felt like I had finally learned how to beat this thing. That magic solution that I wanted in 2003 didn't exist, but I truly believed that I had conquered anxiety disorders and that smooth sailing was in my future. This overconfidence wound up teaching me a lesson about the dangers of becoming less vigilant.

Getting Too Comfortable

For the months that followed that summer, I felt amazing. My anxiety was a fraction of what it used to be, and I felt genuinely healthy for the first time in my life. Years of reading about anxiety and experiencing its symptoms firsthand had brought me to a point in which I felt like I understood the condition and could easily conquer it. In fact, I mistakenly felt that I had conquered it already. Three months of smart decisions had left me in a better place than I'd ever been, and that unfortunately made it easier for me to start slacking on the hard work that it took to get me there.

With my weight already at the 165 goal that I had set at the beginning of the summer, I had no clear exercise goal to shoot for. Clear, quantifiable goals are the key to me getting off the couch and getting things done, as vague attempts to stay in shape never seem to work. I was at my goal weight, but I made the mistake of not deciding on some other fitness goal to strive for (run a 5K, improve my mile pace to a certain time, etc.). This was the stroke of death for my regular fitness routine, and my trips to the rec center became less and less frequent.

My anxiety rarely reared its head during this period, which had the unfortunate side effect of taking away my main motivation to continue my meditation practice. I'd start my timer and try to meditate a couple of times a week, only to abort mid-session and move on about my day. Within no time at all, I had completely stopped meditating and exercising – the two things that were primarily responsible for my newfound freedom from anxiety.

As anyone that's ever had a tendency to "yo-yo" in weight can attest, this led to me gaining back almost all of the weight I had lost within a matter of months. Before I knew it, the status quo was right back to where it was before that productive three-month period. I was fatter, I wasn't exercising or meditating, I was drinking 1,000+ calories of beer on several nights every week, and believe it or not, my anxiety came back.

Not only did it come back, it came back like it had something to prove after staying in the background for all of that time. As was the case before, it really hit me hard on days after heavy drinking. I'm not sure if I was drinking more after the three-month break or if my tolerance had gone down, but those "day after" bouts with anxiety were on a level I hadn't experienced since 2003.

One of the worst experiences came when I went to Chicago with my father for the wedding of my cousin. My dad and I regularly have way too much to drink when we get together, but the open bar on that night ensured that we'd be on another level. A cute friend of the bride asked me to dance with her at one point during the reception, which is something I never do. Being single and attracted to her, however, I decided I should give it a shot. Of course, I quickly downed several drinks of whiskey before I actually got up the nerve to get on the dance floor.

With the reception winding down and the crowd being composed of mostly middle-aged Catholic people, the girl I danced with told me that her friends were going to head out and hit some of the bars in Wrigleyville. I liked the girl and it sounded like a good way to check out some fun spots around the city, so I said my goodbyes to the dwindling reception crowd and we headed out the door.

This is one of the first nights I think about when I'm reminded of why 2am last calls are a good thing. They allow you to have a nice, long night of fun as you bounce around bars, but you can still be in bed early enough to not feel like death the next day. Whenever I'm in a city that doesn't have this (Las Vegas, New Orleans, etc.), the odds of me having a very rough time the next day increase exponentially.

Chicago apparently lets some bars stay open until 5am, so we naturally gravitated towards those. We were already liquored up from the wedding, but the night extended for hours and hours as we took shots and got entirely too inebriated. By 5am, I was drunk enough to allow something to happen that I'm typically very vigilant about. One member of our group offered to drive us back to the hotel, and I accepted the ride despite the fact that he was probably nearly as drunk as me. My memory is hazy of this night, but I remember him making an illegal turn at an intersection. Across the intersection, a police car turned on its lights and started turning to head in our direction. Our driver sped up and started making rapid serpentine turns through the streets of downtown Chicago in an attempt to lose the officer (he eventually did).

My dad still reminds me of the text that he woke up to the next morning: "It's 5am, I'm by the Sears Tower, and I'm probably going to die." I sent that as this pursuit of sorts was going on, and probably half-believed it at the time. Of course, this proved to be a concerning text for a father to read immediately upon waking up (especially considering that I was passed out and not picking up my phone when he tried to call).

We joke about that night now, but the following day was one of the worst I've had in terms of anxiety. I remember numerous, strong panic attacks hitting me throughout the day. One was in a taxi as we headed out to lunch, and a stronger one occurred as we walked around Navy Pier. There were several elements in place that combined to form an intensely trying day. The massive hangover was the main catalyst, but I was also more vulnerable to anxiety when I was in unfamiliar territory. A day at home in my own bed would be bad enough after a night of drinking like that, much less a day of having to go to several tourist destinations in a city that I wasn't familiar with. In addition, I spent the entire day with my father, who had still not put any effort into understanding what anxiety disorders were all about. The combination of feeling miserable and also trying to hide it made things worse, and my dad noticed that something was up. When he saw me clearly struggling to eat and maintain conversation at one point, he said something along the lines of "Are you having some weird anxiety thing? Stop it, just chill out." That didn't help matters.

I made it through the day, but an even worse experience happened just a month later. College was winding down, and my friends and I decided to celebrate with a trip to Las Vegas. Taking in a show or hitting a hot nightclub were never things that interested me in that city, so I immediately saddled up to the craps table at the decidedly seedy Buffalo Bill's casino on the first night. Sleep was always hard to come by in the nights before I flew, so I was already exhausted when I arrived. With the free drinks in Vegas, I decided to remedy this by ordering a steady stream of Red Bull and vodkas (sometimes two at a time). The table was hot and I was having a blast, so I continued rolling the dice late into the night with a Red Bull and vodka constantly at the ready.

What happened later that night should have been the least surprising thing in the world, but I was having too much fun in the moment to think about the consequences. Caffeine had a tendency to raise my anxiety levels, and I had never even tasted energy drinks before that night. Alcohol was a clear culprit when it came to my worst moments of anxiety, and there was plenty of that coming in as well. When you combine those two things with my long history of having trouble sleeping, it's an obvious recipe for disaster.

When I made it back to the hotel, I had no idea that I was in for one of the worst, most prolonged panic attacks I had ever had in my life. Whereas I'd usually experience my symptoms the next day, this instance involved me not being able to sleep thanks to the copious amounts of caffeine. Four of us were sharing a room, and we decided to trade off the nights that we'd get access to the room's two beds. I had lost the coin flip earlier in the day, so this was my night to sleep on the ground.

I laid down on the floor, already buzzing from all of the caffeine and excitement that the last several hours at the craps table had provided. At this point, it was probably four or five in the morning. When I'm drunk, I'm usually able to fall asleep significantly faster than on nights in which I haven't been drinking. This night was different thanks to all of the caffeine, and I laid on the uncomfortable floor of the Excalibur with the silly idea that I'd somehow be able to sleep.

What I experienced was something new to me. Through all of my years of drinking during college, I had always been a beer or straight whiskey guy. With god knows how much Red Bull in my system, this was the first time I had laid down while I was drunk and not been seconds away from being asleep. Buzzing sensations coursed through my head and extremities, which I tried to ignore as I told myself I'd just pass out like always. It didn't stop, and I grew increasingly concerned as I tossed and turned on the thin blanket that covered the hard floor of our cheap room.

Minutes seemed like hours as I tried to quiet my mind long enough to fall asleep, but it wasn't in the cards. I hadn't packed my laptop and I was a couple of years away from owning a smartphone, so I didn't even have anything that could keep me occupied until I fell asleep (I didn't turn on the TV or a light, as I didn't want to wake up my friends). Meditating seemed impossible as my brain continued to speed up, and I started experiencing the onset of a panic attack as it dawned on me that this was likely to be a long night.

My stomach felt fine, but the quickly worsening anxiety made me feel like I was on the verge of vomiting. I rushed to the bathroom and tried to throw up as quietly as possible. Even after my stomach was empty, my intense anxiety kept telling me that I needed to vomit. I dry heaved over and over again as I grew lightheaded and began to see dozens of small white specks appear in front of my eyes. It was a sensation I had never experienced in the almost five years I'd struggled with anxiety, and I had no explanation for why my vision was affected. All I could think was "holy crap, it's never been *this* bad."

My repeated dry heaves eventually woke up my friend Libby, who groggily asked if I was alright. I lied and said that I had just had too much to drink, and she went back to bed. I stepped away from the toilet and sat on the sink counter, burying my head in my hands. All I wanted was for this night to be over, and I remember looking at the hotel clock and realizing that it would be hours until I saw the sun. For some reason, seeing the sun come up always comforted me on nights like these. Something about people getting out of the house and starting their days made me feel less alone, even if I was stuck in a bedroom either way.

I didn't even want to lie back down, as I knew my mind was nowhere near being able to settle. Other options sounded similarly terrible at the time. I could have gone downstairs and gambled a bit, but being around people when I was in this state sounded like too much to handle. With no option sounding like a good solution, I continued sitting on the sink counter in my pajama pants and just hoped that time would pass as quickly as possible.

After several minutes of sitting like this, some disturbing thoughts began to enter my mind. In the worst attacks of my early struggles with anxiety, I often worried that I'd go insane and wind up in a mental institution. At this moment in Las Vegas, I started worrying about losing my mind for the first time in years. I looked out the window of the Excalibur and realized that we were on one of the higher floors of the hotel. At no point in my life have I ever been even close to suicidal, but my mind was in a bad spot at this very moment and I began to worry. What if I truly lost my mind and jumped out the window, despite having no desire to do it? Even in the midst of this awful panic attack, suicide was never something I'd ever come close to considering. But what if the attack worsened and worsened until I wasn't in my right mind anymore and I somehow jumped?

It was a ludicrous thought, but it worried me regardless in my condition. I grabbed my phone, slipped on some shoes, and left the room. All I wanted was to be away from any option to hurt myself in the event that I actually went crazy, so I took the elevator down to the casino floor. The lights and sounds of the slot machines were way too much to handle in my current state, so I wandered the hotel until I found a relatively quiet space near the halls reserved for business meetings.

I sat down and decided that the best way to pass the time and ease my state of mind would be to call someone close to me and talk about what was going on. It was probably 5am in Vegas, so my family and friends in Kansas would be close to getting up. My mother was starting to learn more about anxiety, but I didn't want to worry her about what I was going through on that night. My father wasn't an option, as he was still stubborn about sympathizing with my condition. I had the numbers of several doctors' offices in my phone, but those were for making appointments. I landed on the girl that I was dating when I had trouble swallowing my food at Applebee's. We had broken up at this point, but it was amicable and she was one of the few people that really knew about what I was going through. In addition, she was about to graduate with a degree in pharmacy, so she'd know more about the medical aspects of this than me.

She was understandably surprised to hear from me considering that we hadn't seen each other in months, but she could tell that I was in a tough spot and took the time to talk me through it. I explained every aspect of the night to her, and she stayed on the line with me and remained understanding for quite a while. When we eventually ended our conversation, I felt considerably better. It was just another example of how opening up to those close to you can only help matters.

I made my way back up to the room and laid on the floor once again. Even though I didn't feel great by any means, the conversation had calmed me somewhat and my brain was exhausted from the past few hours. I managed to fall asleep, and the worst was behind me. The next day was by no means easy, but the dread of that night had lessened in the light of day as I was surrounded by my friends.

Despite not feeling great, I survived the rest of the trip (while consciously abstaining from excessive alcohol use) and headed back to Kansas for my final semester of college. My anxiety stuck with me for those remaining months, and I knew that a new challenge was on the horizon as I graduated and moved out into the real world.

DAN RYCKERT

Anxiety In The Real World

The one-two punch of Chicago and Las Vegas had made it clear to me that I had not "conquered" anxiety (I'd learn later that there was really no such thing). Two of my worst experiences with anxiety had occurred after I had become confident that I had beaten it for good, so this was bound to be a longer fight than I had hoped. Compounding my anxiety was the fact that I was about to be done with college and thrust out into the real world.

My plan throughout college was that I'd coast my way through my easy Film Studies classes enough to get a degree, while spending most of my time reviewing video games on the side for a local newspaper in an effort to build a portfolio. After years of doing this, I had amassed over 600 video game reviews that I could show to any outlet that had an open position. Problem is, most video game media outlets didn't have much in the way of turnover. Open positions were infrequent, and employers would be bombarded with applications and resumes the second a rare one would open up.

Throughout college, I applied to every open position I saw from any gaming outlet I had ever heard of. I went through numerous interviews, but was repeatedly told to get back in touch with them after I had gotten my degree. Once I graduated, I had plenty of contacts within the industry but there were no open positions to shoot for.

In the weeks before I was set to move back to Kansas City from Lawrence (my college town), I spent a lot of time debating what I should do. My degree was in Film Studies, but I had seen too many friends move to LA and hate everything about it (I hated the city myself after several years of flying there for the annual E3 convention). I had a ton of experience in gaming journalism and a degree in Film Studies, but I couldn't figure out how to turn either of those things into a full-time job.

I've always had a desire to shoot for the best possible scenario for myself, so I hated the idea of settling on anything. That said, I was forced to settle considering the situation I was in. A close friend of mine from high school had graduated a year before me and started working for a local Kansas City sports station. I was never much of a sports guy, but the position was relevant to my degree and part of me really liked the idea of working in live television. I talked to the station manager and he offered me a position that would pay $19,000 a year with no medical insurance or other benefits.

This was 2008, and $19,000 was woefully under the median pay in Kansas City. My friends were graduating with engineering degrees and immediately making $55,000 out of college, while I was accepting a job that was somewhat tied to my major but paid barely enough to afford rent. That said, live TV experience would look good on my resume and I decided to make the most out of it. I accepted the job, and started my crash course in how to help run a live television program.

All of my previous relevant experience had focused on directing, editing, and writing, so I had little knowledge of how to run audio boards, build graphics, or deal with problems on the fly during a live broadcast. Editing highlight reels of various sporting events resembled my previous experience enough to be easy, but everything in the control room during a live broadcast was foreign to me. I wanted to learn everything, so I would ask the audio and graphics guys to let me shadow them during live broadcasts so that I could be more versatile at the station (ideally leading to a raise at some point).

I learned the mechanics of running an audio board and Chyron (a system for making graphics such as lower-thirds) quickly, but that didn't prepare me for the pressure that immediately built up in me once one of our shows went live. Monitoring microphone levels and building lower third graphics was no problem on paper, but it became a different beast once the red light was on. It would have been easy if it was just a matter of performing the relevant job functions, but the struggle came from within my head.

Every time we were on the air, I'd imagine the doomsday scenario of my anxiety becoming so overwhelming that I'd have to leave the room. It never actually happened, but that didn't stop my fear. I just knew that one of these days, it'd be too much and I'd be forced to abandon my post and leave the control room (ruining the broadcast and likely being fired). It was a similar sensation to what I'd feel when I was sitting on a plane or in the middle of a packed theater row – if I couldn't easily get up, walk out, and get a breather, it meant I was in for surefire anxiety. Live television provided the height of this feeling, as the consequences of abandoning a broadcast were far worse than anything I'd experienced before.

One example of an anxiety-provoking situation during a show was actually a pretty funny one. It was early on in my time at the station, and someone had instructed me on the correct audio tracks to play during college basketball highlights. I wanted to make sure that I didn't screw anything up, so I wrote down each acceptable track and printed out a quick reference sheet that I could post on the wall in the audio booth. What the producer neglected to tell me is that these tracks were on one particular CD. I assumed that I'd just have to queue up the right track on the CD player prior to the segment airing, and press play at the right time. When the anchors tossed to the highlights, I made sure I was on the right track number, hit play, and brought up the music levels. Within seconds, I realized that something was seriously wrong. Instead of fast-paced electronic music accompanying the University of Kansas basketball highlights, the anchors were talking over a repeated audio loop of a horse wildly neighing (a "barnyard sounds" CD was in the player for some reason). They attempted to ignore it as they gave play-by-play over a couple of clips, but eventually addressed it live on the air. Our lead anchor said "I'm not sure what's going on in the audio booth, but we're apparently airing our salute to Barbaro during these KU highlights" (Barbaro was a thoroughbred racehorse that had been euthanized a year earlier). My anxiety immediately spiked as I scrambled to find the correct disc, but the segment ended before I had a chance to locate it.

A less funny incident made more of an impact on me a couple of weeks later. I had never run the teleprompter during a broadcast, as it was an extremely simple task that was typically left to interns with little experience. When our interns weren't available during one broadcast, the producers looked to the new guy (me) and asked if I'd take over for one of our shows. Running audio or Chyron was far more complicated and stressful, so I assumed running the prompter would be a cakewalk. On a technical level, it was. My job was to sit just off-camera and rotate a circular knob at a pace that would allow the anchors to read the scrolling text off their monitors. It's a task that a 12 year-old should be able to perform with no issues whatsoever.

It was a simple enough job as it was, but it was made even easier thanks to the fact that one particular segment would be filmed ahead of time (eliminating the possibility of a doomsday scenario in which I left and ruined a live broadcast). One of our shows always ended with a pre-taped rant in which our lead anchor would speak for three or four minutes about something in the world of Kansas City sports that was particularly irking him that day. I don't remember what he was talking about on this specific episode, but he was struggling with getting through a few lines of his script. I'd slowly rotate the teleprompter knob as he worked his way through the text, only to reset it to the beginning once he stumbled over his words and we had to start over.

This didn't bother me for the first few times. Teleprompter work was idiot-proof, and all it required was the ability to rotate a knob at the same pace that the anchor talked. Despite the simplicity of the task, I found myself becoming increasingly nervous every time that our anchor flubbed a line and had to start over. I knew that I wasn't doing anything wrong, but I started feeling a variety of symptoms that let me know that I wanted to get out of there as soon as possible.

This continued over and over, and I started feeling my right hand involuntarily shake. It made no sense to me, as I had all the confidence in the world that I could accomplish this simple task. No amount of confidence could stop my mounting anxiety, however, and it got worse and worse every time the anchor misread a line and had to start over. After ten or fifteen minutes of repeated attempts, I started to seriously wonder if I'd be able to handle much more of this. My brain was screaming at me to get out of there, and I started worrying about the repercussions if I had to simply stand up and leave the studio.

I forced myself to stay, but my hands started shaking more and more as he continued to flub his lines. It was easy to explain anxiety during live broadcasts to myself, but I was shocked to find myself getting so anxious during a pre-taped segment. At one point, I remember grabbing my right wrist with my left hand in an effort to steady it so that I could maintain control of the teleprompter knob. By the time he actually got through the entire segment, my vision was starting to get dark around the edges and my entire body was buzzing. Afterwards, I had to sit down in my car for a good fifteen minutes just to calm down before I started driving home.

From that moment forward, I had an irrational fear of being asked to run the teleprompter. I'd perform far more complicated duties like running the audio board or Chyron on a daily basis without too much of a problem, but I'd start to panic if I knew they were looking for a prompter operator for the day or even one segment. I'd go into the restroom and wait for several minutes, hoping they would ask some intern or other editor to do it.

Turning the knob wasn't what scared me. What scared me was the idea of a repeat of what happened during that first night on teleprompter duty. I pictured myself buckling under the pressure and leaving the studio, instantly being fired in a time that I couldn't afford to be out of a job. It was another example of being hit by the fear of fear, not the fear of performing a simple task that I was overqualified to do.

I had never once left a live broadcast as it was in progress, even on occasions that my panic was peaking. Regardless of my 100% success rate in the past, the fear persisted and started to seep into my other job duties. Running the audio board became a struggle, as did running Chyron. Editing video packages together prior to the shows was the only time that I felt like I wasn't on the verge of a massive attack. I'd look at the schedule each week, and immediately start to worry if I saw myself in any key role for long live shows. My symptoms rose up every day as I'd look at the clock and see it marching closer to showtime. If I didn't improve my situation quickly, I wouldn't be able to continue at this job much longer. Nothing else was lined up if I left the TV station, as there were few similar jobs in the area and the gaming outlets that I wanted to work for didn't have any openings.

My low pay didn't allow me luxuries like a gym membership, and I didn't put any real effort into finding alternative cheap ways to exercise. I neglected to jump back into meditation for some reason, which is insane considering it's free, simple, and had proved to be highly effective just a year earlier. Instead, I found a psychologist that operated on a sliding scale since I didn't have any health insurance.

The last time I had seen a psychologist was in the early years of my condition, so there was a lot to catch up on. I explained my history and my current situation, and he seemed surprised that I'd voluntarily go into an industry as inherently high-stress as live television. He specialized in patients with anxiety, and had heard tons of stories that resembled my fear of running the teleprompter. Any situation that provokes a strong panic attack can become a repeated trigger of symptoms, and these situations vary wildly from person to person.

He told me a story of one of his patients, a woman that was terrified of going to the grocery store. On one occasion before she had this problem, she dropped a large bag of groceries on the ground as she left the store and they scattered everywhere. As she picked them up while others in line looked at her, she became increasingly self-conscious until things eventually escalated into a full-blown panic attack. Ever since then, she refused to step foot in a grocery store.

His advice to her was simple. She was to go to the grocery store the next day, buy a ton of groceries, and drop them on purpose as she left the store. Of course, this sounded like an insane proposition to her. Was this psychologist really suggesting that she voluntarily put herself in the exact situation she feared more than anything?

He explained the concept of cognitive behavioral therapy (CBT), a common approach that essentially boils down to forcing yourself to confront your fear. Once she had done this and come out the other side unscathed, the boogeyman of this fear would be less scary in the future. She listened to his advice and dropped her groceries the next day. It was a scary event for her as she headed into the grocery store, but this specific fear was diminished significantly after going through with it.

It's a tactic that makes sense, and if you go the other way, you run the risk of your world getting smaller. Let's say I had a similar fear of the grocery store and refused to go there any more. Then let's say I had a panic attack on the highway and refused to stop driving on it. After that, maybe I have a panic attack while at a sporting event and vow never to return to one. If that's the path you go down, your world shrinks and shrinks until you're essentially agoraphobic and afraid to leave your house.

This seemed like a scary road to go down, so I vowed to attack my fears head-on in the future. From then on, the more scared I was of something, the more prone I was to do it. This has been a critical decision for me in my treatment, and it's one that I remind myself of on a regular basis.

My first opportunity to put this new attitude in place was the next day at work. I was anxious on the drive there, as my plan was to immediately volunteer myself as the teleprompter operator as soon as the producers started making the rounds and looking for one. This approach was a far cry from the days I hid in the bathroom, but I was confident that it was the right thing to do for my long-term health.

Fifteen minutes before we went live, I saw my producer sit up from her desk and start walking towards the control room of the studio. Typically, she'd approach an intern on the way and ask if they'd run prompter. Instead, I intercepted her and asked if she had anyone lined up yet. She said no, and I told her I'd be happy to do it since I wasn't scheduled for any other role that day. This probably surprised her, as I had been miraculously disappearing during this specific part of the day for weeks now. She thanked me for the offer and told me that I was on prompter for one of our half-hour live shows.

The last time I was on prompter, it triggered a massive panic attack even though the segment was pre-taped. Doing it live was a far scarier proposal. I felt the symptoms appear the second I walked into the studio, and tried to keep my cool as I chatted with the anchors prior to showtime. When the thirty second countdown started, I could already feel my extremities start to tingle. My feet and hands felt like they were on the verge of falling asleep, which concerned me considering that I wouldn't be of much help without full use of my hands.

When I ran prompter, I always hated the first segment of the shows the most. That was the most script-heavy for the anchors, as the show would focus more on video packages and casual conversation in later segments. I stared at the wall of text on the monitor in front of me, and tried to focus on keeping the script scrolling at the right speed instead of focusing on my mounting panic. Even in this state, I knew how ridiculous it was that my body was reacting that way. Literally all I had to do was turn a knob as I read a screen. I could have done this job when I was a child, and it probably would have been easier back then considering I didn't have panic to worry about yet.

When the first commercial break hit, I felt a brief wave of relief. I wasn't out of the woods yet, but I could chug some water to soothe my dry throat and give my mind a quick break after seven or eight minutes of trying to focus intensely. The next two segments of the show went as expected, with my panic spiking whenever I was approaching a large chunk of script.

During these moments, I thought of something else the psychologist told me. He mentioned that there's always a defined peak to these attacks. They can get very, very intense, but there's a certain limit as to how far a panic attack can go. It's not like an attack was going to increase in strength exponentially until I was pulling my hair out and rolling around on the ground. I kept this in mind, along with my usual "it always ends" reminder. Looking at the clock, I kept thinking "in a matter of minutes, this will all be over. I'll get in my car, I'll be safe, and I can just go home and relax."

Sure enough, I made it through. No bolting out of the room, no getting fired, and no complete loss of control of my hands. It was a tough half-hour, but the anxiety peaked and then it ended. When the show went off the air, I felt an immediate sense of relaxation come over my body in a wave. I let out a long breath, stood up, and felt like I had just won a prizefight. On the outside, I had slightly rotated a knob for thirty minutes while looking at text on a screen. Inside, I had an immense feeling of satisfaction after conquering a fear that had been plaguing me for weeks. I walked out to my car and couldn't stop smiling, feeling like a million bucks for the entire drive home.

The Worst Year

A variety of factors led to me deciding to leave the TV station, but the regular occurrences of anxiety were at the top of the list. I was able to get that brief victory on the night that I volunteered for prompter duty, but I felt like the long-term war wasn't worth fighting at this employer. The pay was terrible, I had no benefits, I didn't have a passion for sports, my boss was an absolute idiot, and the staff's morale levels were nonexistent. After securing my next job, I gave my two weeks and called it quits.

That next job was better in several ways, but I still felt as if I had been defeated by my anxiety. I shouldn't have been so hard on myself considering that the TV job was terrible even if I was fully mentally healthy, but I couldn't stop thinking that I had lost a battle. While the symptoms were scarier and more mysterious when they first hit me in 2003, at least I was an 18 year-old kid with the excitement of college and gainful employment ahead of me. In late 2008, I was 24 years old and nearly a year out of college, and I had no long-term prospects for a career. This worry coupled with my anxiety at the time to create a rough combination.

I interviewed for and landed a job at Garmin, an automotive GPS company based in Kansas City. My job duties would involve doing basic tech support for products that I didn't really care about, but at least I'd be making a more-reasonable $30,000 a year and would have solid health insurance for once. It didn't take long to learn that live television wasn't the core problem here, as plenty of little situations triggered my attacks even in an environment that shouldn't be nearly as stressful.

For two or three weeks before we'd actually be on the phones doing support, Garmin had every new employee go through training. This involved repeated eight-hour days of staring at incredibly boring PowerPoint slides that taught us about satellite positioning or how to do a hard reset on GPS devices. Every once in a while, my boredom would be interrupted by a spike of anxiety as our trainers would start calling on the new employees (there were about eight in my "class") to answer questions in front of everyone. The TV station might have involved more extreme panic attacks, but at least there I was confined to my little audio booth or teleprompter station. Here, I was forced to talk in front of a group for the first time since the stressful introductions at my college call center job.

These long days of alternating between sheer boredom and sudden anxiety started wearing on me quickly, and I decided that it might be time to give prescription medication another shot. It had been many years since my brief usage of Paxil, and I knew more about medication now. Every medication works differently for everyone, and I didn't even take the Paxil long enough for its potentially positive effects to be felt.

Unfortunately, my insurance wouldn't kick in until I was at the company for three months. St. John's Wort and other remedies hadn't worked in the past, but I wanted a temporary experiment while I waited for insurance. While I was at the grocery store, I saw a flavor of Vitamin Water that claimed to aid in relaxation. I knew that it was probably BS, but I hoped that my dumb brain would allow the placebo effect to work some kind of magic until I got actual medication. Every day, I'd sit in training with a bottle of this Vitamin Water and try to tell myself that it was having an effect. At one point, I decided to bypass the liquid part of it and narrow in on what was supposedly the active ingredient. The bottle claimed that it was an amino acid called theanine that provided the "relaxing" effects of the drink, so I picked up a bottle of capsules and started taking them daily.

It's obvious that the placebo effect is real in a wide variety of studies, but just *hoping* that my brain would be fooled didn't prove to be an effective remedy. I knew going in that the Vitamin Water and theanine capsules wouldn't make any actual difference, so the experiment was doomed from the start. Lesson learned.

As I'd sit through these training days and eventually move on to actual work, I dreaded every second I was in that office. The company itself was fine and did its best to try to make its employees happy, but I couldn't shake the idea that I should be doing so much more than a call center job. That job at Garmin is something that anyone with any level of technical proficiency could get hired for directly out of high school, so I started wondering if my college degree would actually help me in any way (on a professional level...college had an undeniably positive impact on my social life). I had always been confident that I'd wind up doing something I loved for a living, just as long as I remained focused and persistent no matter what.

Working in gaming journalism was the end goal, and I had continued writing for the Lawrence Journal-World newspaper even after graduating college and moving back to Kansas City. Finding time to review every notable video game release wasn't easy when I was also working a full-time position at Garmin, but I knew it would be necessary if I wanted to get a leg up on the thousands of other prospective writers. I worked the night shift, so I'd play video games from the time I woke up until the time I went to work at 3pm, then I'd try to get the reviews written after I got home around midnight. I'm not going to act like playing video games and writing about them is backbreaking work, but the time commitment during this period of my life meant that I didn't have much time for anything else.

One thing that I did find time to do was make a dumb decision that would dump months of wholly avoidable anxiety on my head. When I had started at the sports station, a producer pulled me into an edit room and said "you've gotta watch this." He proceeded to show me a three-minute clip of baseball legend George Brett as he was miked up for a spring training segment for our station. Knowing full well that he had a microphone on his shirt, he followed young Kansas City Royals around the diamond while regaling them with stories about how often he craps his pants ("I'm good twice a year for that," he says proudly). I couldn't stop laughing at the absurdity of this sports legend boasting about crapping his pants at the Bellagio after eating a bunch of crab legs, and the producer gave me a DVD copy of the clip.

Once I had left the TV station for Garmin, I determined that it was my comedic duty to expose the internet to this gem. I uploaded it to YouTube, and it tallied up millions of hits overnight. Every major sports blog in the country was writing about it and linking to it, and even non-sports websites were putting it on their front page. I knew that the clip would draw some attention, but I assumed that it would mostly come from the Kansas City sports crowd. Instead, it was quickly passed around and featured nationwide.

Within a couple of days, the Kansas City Star featured a story about the infamous clip. They had interviewed representatives of the TV station that I had worked for, claiming that the video was "stolen from their vault" and that they'd be pursuing the maximum penalty allowed by law once they found out who leaked it. Considering that I assumed that the video would become a local joke at most, I started worrying when I saw it pop up in the papers with quotes like that.

Things escalated thanks to several updates in the Kansas City Star, and I'd get a ton of phone calls whenever my friends saw the stories ("Hey man, they're saying that they have a good idea of who did it. Are you worried?"). At its peak, TMZ ran highlights of the clip on their national television show and featured a segment where its correspondents talked about the "manhunt" for whoever "stole the clip from the Time Warner vault."

Even though I hadn't stolen anything, I was really starting to panic about what kind of penalty I'd face when or if they found out it was me. I started contacting lawyers so that I could get a better understanding of what to expect. Every morning, I'd look at my phone and dread seeing that I had numerous missed calls or text messages. One of those mornings, I stepped outside to see an overnight FedEx package on my front step. It was from an executive at Time Warner, and the letter informed me that they were aware that I leaked the video. I was told to return any copies of the clip in my possession, and take down anything that was hosted online. The second part of that request was impossible, as my original clip had been taken down by a copyright notice, but tons of reposts had gone up in its place. In addition, parody videos, autotune remixes, and even loving recreations from high school baseball teams were being posted at an alarming speed. This thing had gotten big, and they knew it was me.

I called up the Time Warner exec whose name was on the mailing, and admitted that I had leaked the video. When I attempted to explain to him that I just found the clip really funny and wanted to share it with the internet, his response made me laugh: "Look, Dan…no one is denying that the video is funny."

In the end, I fell back on my policy of being honest and open regardless of the situation. I wrote a letter to my former bosses at the TV station, apologizing for my "immature" decision and owning responsibility. The station director thanked me for being honest, and said that I had made the right call in reaching out to him. No charges were filed, and the situation ended as amicably as I could have hoped for. Despite the fact that I had avoided a court appearance, those months took their toll on me considering the high level of daily anxiety that the situation brought about. Making it worse was the fact that it was entirely avoidable. That said, I stand by the fact that the video is *really* funny.

I got past that situation, but I was still in the roughest period of my life thanks to my mounting anxiety and dissatisfaction with my career situation. Unfortunately, another element was in play that ramped things up more than ever. At 24, I was in my first actual relationship and it wasn't exactly an easy one. The girl I was with suffered from a variety of severe psychological conditions, and they seemed to worsen every month. I tried to get her to seek help for her issues, but she refused to seek treatment. Eventually, the relationship was taking its toll on me to such a point that I had to end it.

For the next year after I broke up with her, she would reappear in my life at random times in increasingly scary ways. With the state of her mental well-being in such a precarious spot, I constantly worried about when she'd show up next and what she was capable of doing. I changed phone numbers, set email filters to avoid her messages, contacted police, and blocked her on all forms of social media, but her constant creation of new email addresses and online accounts ensured that there would be no easy way to avoid her attempts to contact me online or in the real world. Throughout this period of time, my anxiety level stayed at the most sustained high I've ever been through.

I originally wrote this chapter with much more detail in regards to this situation, while still taking measures to keep her anonymous. In the end, I opted to delete the full story and keep it vague. Her situation was far more severe than my anxiety issues, and I wouldn't feel confident writing about mental illnesses that I can't claim to understand or have any experience with.

This period made me want to understand other conditions beyond those that I was diagnosed with. It was staggering to see how bad things could be for those worse off than me, and I wanted to learn whatever I could about them. I was left with a lot more sympathy for people that I might have just dismissed as "crazy" if I hadn't learned more about the causes behind mental illness and psychotic behavior

Fighting mental illness is a matter of finding what works for you, and at this point in my life it was time to focus on finding (and sticking to) the things that worked for me.

DAN RYCKERT

New Avenues

In January of 2009, my insurance through Garmin had gone active and I was finally able to consider prescription medication again. During the first meeting with a new psychiatrist, he acted like my case was no different than god knows how many anxiety sufferers he had seen in his years of practice. I tried to detail the last six years of my condition in the thought that it might differ from the usual patient, but he shrugged it off and wrote me a prescription for buspirone, a drug that specializes in the treatment of generalized anxiety disorder.

In addition, he wrote me a prescription for alprazolam (commonly known as Xanax). I was willing to be on board for the buspirone, but the little I knew about Xanax scared me. In reading about various mental illnesses, I had frequently heard about the highly addictive qualities of the drug. I had heard many people refer to it as being almost too effective at treating panic attacks, especially considering how quickly it takes effect (within an hour of one dose, typically).

My fear was that I'd quickly become an addict. With frequent panic attacks and near omnipresent generalized anxiety at this time, I was afraid that I'd be reaching for a pill on a frequent basis until I eventually became dependent on it. I expressed my concern to the doctor, and he explained to me that he didn't think I exhibited any of the signs of being prone to addiction ("actual addicts don't express any worry over getting addicted to medication…they just want it no matter what," he explained). The buspirone was for daily use, but he said I could view the Xanax as "a fire extinguisher on the wall."

That phrasing has stuck with me ever since he said it. Simply knowing that a fire extinguisher is in your building leads to a certain level of comfort, as you have an effective solution at the ready in case your kitchen is suddenly ablaze. Similarly, just knowing that my "fire extinguisher" was available provided a certain level of comfort without even taking it. I bought a little pill container that goes on a keychain, and I've carried it around with me every day since that appointment. I can't remember the last time I took Xanax (it's probably been two years or more at this point), but it's still nice to know that I have a remedy in my pocket in case a catastrophic panic attack pops up in an unexpected situation.

I went to the pharmacy after that appointment and had both the buspirone and Xanax filled. While I wouldn't take my first dose of the latter for many months, I started my small daily dose of the former on the next morning.

Years prior to this, I made the mistake of not giving Paxil the proper time to become effective. This time around, I told myself that I'd stay on the buspirone for a full three months regardless of how rocky it was at the beginning. Right away, I started noticing a distinct effect that would set in approximately an hour after taking my twice-daily recommended dose. I'd be sitting at work, and a wave of drowsiness would descend on me. I wasn't just sleepy, as I'd feel out of it in a way that was similar to the zombie-like effects of the Paxil back in the early days of my condition.

Working at this call center was already making me feel like I wasn't where I was meant to be at that point in my life, and the effects of the buspirone made it feel even more like I was just treading water. My days were a cycle of getting up, playing a few games for review, taking my buspirone before work, spending hours feeling like a zombie, only to take my second dose and get hit by the feeling once again. I'd get home and get some writing done before going to bed and waking up to repeat the process all over again. For a guy that has always prided himself on staying excitable and positive even during trying times, I felt like I was gradually being removed from my natural state by a combination of uninspiring work and the wrong medication.

I gave buspirone the three months that I told myself I would, and I tapered myself off of it as soon as that period was over. This time, I knew that I gave it a real shot and didn't cut things off prematurely. Again, buspirone (like Paxil) may work for others but it certainly wasn't doing anything to help me. It wasn't lessening my anxiety, it was just dulling the rest of my day to an uncomfortable degree. For a couple of months, the only medication that I had was my "fire extinguisher" Xanax that I never actually took.

By June of 2009, I was still in the midst of dealing with my ex-girlfriend's repeated attempts to contact me and my growing disappointment in my professional life while I was in Los Angeles for the gaming industry's annual E3 convention. I always tried to stay optimistic and have fun, so I decided to do something that I had wanted to do since I was a kid. As long as I could remember, late night comedy had been a staple of my daily (well, nightly) life. I looked forward to Friday nights as a kid as it was the only night I was allowed to stay up late enough to watch David Letterman with my father. As I got older, Conan O'Brien became a major favorite of mine.

2009's E3 convention lined up perfectly with Conan taking over *The Tonight Show,* so it couldn't have been a better time to see him live. I called up NBC's ticket line prior to the trip and secured a ticket for his third show behind the legendary desk. My excitement about seeing one of my lifelong idols live took me out of the cloud of anxiety that I had been engulfed in for over a year, albeit temporarily.

As the crowd shuffled into the studio after waiting outside for about two hours, a comedian came out with the task of warming up the crowd and letting them know the rules of the taping. I felt nothing but excitement until he stressed that once the show starts, no one can leave their seats. He said that if we had any interest in stepping outside or going to the bathroom, we had one last chance to do it before the show started.

Just like that, I felt the familiar sense of panic that popped up whenever I was confined to a middle seat in a movie theater aisle. I immediately started dreaming up worst-case scenarios, most of which involved me scrambling out of the studio while everyone watched me screw up the taping of one of my idol's shows.

After a couple of minutes, the opening comedian primed the audience and told them to start applauding as soon as the band started playing the intro music. A timer counted down from ten, and Max Weinberg and his band started playing the theme music at its conclusion. The "applause" sign lit up, and the studio came alive as everyone started clapping. I managed to clap for a few seconds until I realized that there was no turning back at this point. I was locked in to this seat for at least an hour, and it was going to be terribly embarrassing if I had to get up and step outside. It took no time at all for this uneasy feeling to escalate into a full-scale panic attack.

For the first time, I decided to turn to my fire extinguisher. I took my keychain out of my pocket, and had trouble unscrewing the little bottle with hands that were shaking at this point. By the time the theme song ended, I had half of a 0.50mg pill of Xanax in my hand. I immediately realized that I didn't have any water and that my mouth was bone dry from the anxiety, so this wasn't going to be pleasant.

I discreetly slipped the pill into my mouth and tried to swallow it. My trouble with swallowing combined with the lack of liquid in my mouth, so it repeatedly popped back up onto my tongue. The taste of the pill wasn't pleasant, and I was worried that I looked insane as I frantically and repeatedly tried to swallow it. After several attempts, it finally went down.

At this point, my brain moved on to something else to worry about. Having never actually tried the Xanax in the several months I had been prescribed it, I had no idea what to expect. The prescription told me to take 0.50mg twice a day, and here I was worried about taking 0.25mg once. I had smoked pot a handful of times in college and never really liked the feeling of being high, and I was worried that this would be a similar sensation that would heighten my anxiety instead of treating it.

For the monologue portion of Conan's act, I was a mixture of physically uncomfortable thanks to the gross taste in my dry mouth, while mentally bracing myself for the unknown effects of the Xanax. By the time Conan's first guest (Julia Louis-Dreyfus) arrived on the couch, the effects had definitely started to set in.

It blew me away to experience my anxiety wash away in such a short amount of time. Despite the effectiveness of the drug's intended purpose, it came with an unfortunate side effect. I was finally doing something that I had wanted to do for years, and I caught myself nodding off. This day was coming off of a night of good sleep and I hadn't been tired previously, but the Xanax made it genuinely difficult to stay awake.

By the time Bradley Cooper came out as the second guest, I was physically starting to nod off in the audience. As I write this, I'm looking at a description of that episode and am just learning that Sheryl Crow performed at the end. I have no memory of this performance whatsoever.

I went from being excited in line to having a panic attack during the intro to literally falling asleep by the end of the episode. Part of me was thankful that I had avoided a panic attack, but a larger part was concerned at the consequences. My anxiety had disappeared, but I also lost a good chunk of what should have been a great experience that I had looked forward to for years.

If I had already been wary of Xanax when the doctor prescribed it to me, that concern increased tenfold after I realized how effective it was. Right away, I understood how easy it must be for people in my situation to spiral into dependency. After all, it was a nearly immediate remedy for a terribly difficult problem. If I turned to a pill every time I felt a tinge of anxiety, I worried that I'd be just a year or two away from being interviewed under a bridge on A&E's *Intervention*.

I decided that I'd continue carrying the "fire extinguisher," but promise myself that I'd only use it when absolutely necessary. Despite being prescribed

0.50mg twice a day, I couldn't fathom doing that when half of that dose nearly knocked me out. As enticing as a life without panic sounded, it didn't seem like a desirable trade-off if I'd just be sleepwalking through my days. I'm writing this nearly six years after that Conan taping, and I've probably only taken Xanax (always at the 0.25mg dose) on less than ten occasions. It's powerful, it's effective, and it can easily become dangerous if usage is left unchecked. My doctors have consistently told me that I don't need to be so steadfast on this opinion ("I prescribed this to you for a reason" is something I've been told more than once), but my gut has kept me away from it unless it's in the most dire of situations.

Upon returning to Kansas City, I knew that it was time to try out another daily option since keeping with a regular Xanax schedule wasn't going to happen. Neither Paxil nor buspirone had worked at all for me, but I wasn't ready to give up. Hoping that the third time was the charm, I went to a doctor and left the office with a prescription for sertraline (Zoloft). I was to take 12.5mg a day for a week, and then 25mg a day after that. After about six weeks, the doctor told me to come back in and we'd discuss bumping the dose up further.

I'm glad that I chose to give this a shot when I did, because my appointment was just days before the first death of a close relative that I'd ever experienced. Growing up, I was always extremely close to my father's parents. I stayed with them frequently, and my grandmother had always been one of the most loving people I had ever had the pleasure of knowing. On June 13th, 2009, she passed away after a battle with esophageal cancer. Just two days earlier, I was lucky enough to have one final great conversation with her as I sat bedside in her hospital room.

The news of her passing was expected, but anyone who has been through the death of a close relative can attest to it having a major impact on one's mental health. I was happy for all the great memories she had given me as well as being happy about that last conversation, but her passing had a definite effect on my anxiety during this already-difficult time.

With the process of introducing Zoloft into my system already in effect, I hoped that it would work and eventually get me out of the rut I had been in ever since leaving college. That trip to Los Angeles proved to be important not just for the Conan taping, as another event happened that would have much more of a lasting impact on my life.

Back in the Fight

During that trip to E3 in Los Angeles, I accomplished my yearly goal of tracking down the editor-in-chief of Game Informer magazine. Writing for the magazine had been my goal ever since I first subscribed at the age of nine after seeing it next to the register when I bought Mortal Kombat for the Sega Genesis.

My relationship with Game Informer had already been years in the making by the time the 2009 E3 rolled around. I began working at a GameStop location at the age of 16 in 2000, and GameStop was Game Informer's parent company. After a couple of years of working there, I had an idea for how to get in touch with the magazine's staff. I called the company's Texas headquarters and offered to shoot a television commercial for them for free if they'd fly me up to Minneapolis to shoot it at Game Informer's headquarters. Somehow, they agreed and I spent a week hanging out with the staff as I shot the TV spot. The entire reason I pitched the commercial idea was so that I could see what day-to-day life was like at the magazine I wanted to work for, and that week cemented my desire to reach that goal.

Once I started writing about video games in college, I paid my way out to E3 every year and made it a goal to run into as many Game Informer editors as I could. Whenever I did, I'd introduce myself as "that kid that shot that commercial back in 2003," and explain that I was now writing about video games and wanted to work for the magazine. Positions in gaming journalism don't see a lot of turnover, so I was told each year that there were no openings.

Running into Andy McNamara (GI's editor-in-chief) at E3 2009 was the first time I received a different answer than the one I had grown used to. I spotted him leaving a Nintendo press conference, and he interrupted me before I could even spout off my usual introduction. "Yeah, I know...you're Dan, the kid that shot the commercial," he said. I let him know that I had written over 600 game reviews at this point and still wanted to work for him, and he mentioned that some spots might be opening soon. Game Informer was about to revamp their magazine and online presence, and they'd be hiring new editors as a result.

After years of flat-out "we have no openings" responses, I was ecstatic to hear that things might be changing soon. Once I was back in Kansas City, I waited impatiently for news regarding the openings. Every email or phone call that I received that wasn't regarding the position annoyed me, as it was all I could think about at the time.

About a month after E3, I woke up to an email from Andy saying that they were starting to get some movement on their end and they wanted a copy of my resume and several writing samples. I jumped out of bed and ran to my computer, opening up a list of my favorite articles that I had prepared for exactly this situation. After spending a few minutes re-reading my cover letter and resume, I replied with my writing samples and went right back to playing the waiting game.

After almost two years of post-college disappointment in my professional life, I finally felt excitement come roaring back. This was the moment that I had kept waiting for during all of those years of writing video game reviews for free, and I was certain that the job was mine.

With all of this excitement, it was a good time for the Zoloft's effects to start kicking in. To my surprise, I reacted in an entirely different way than I had with Paxil or buspirone. Namely, it worked. I'm sure that the optimism and excitement brought about by the job opportunity didn't hurt, but I found myself significantly less anxious on a day-to-day basis as I waited for the final word from Game Informer.

During my follow-up visit to the doctor, he asked me how things were going. I said that things were great – my anxiety was lower than it had been in years, and I wasn't even noticing any negative side effects. He responded by saying I should up my Zoloft dosage to 50mg instead of the 25mg I had been on for these initial weeks. I thought about it and told him that I didn't think it was necessary. If this was how I felt on 25mg, then I didn't feel any need to arbitrarily increase the amount of medication I was taking.

In the morning after a long night at my favorite Shawnee, Kansas dive bar, I woke up to a phone call from a Minnesota area code. Sure enough, it was the executive editor of Game Informer. I immediately got out of bed and began pacing around my house as I waited to hear the words that I had wanted to hear since I was nine years old. They finally came – Game Informer wanted to hire me on as an associate editor, and asked how long it would take me to move up to Minneapolis.

Any anxiety over this major life change would have to wait until later, as pure adrenaline was rushing through me as the details of the hiring process were explained to me. I'd have to take a pay cut from my job at Garmin, but I didn't care a single bit if I was going to be doing something that I loved. Typical job etiquette would have me saying I'd "think about the offer and get back to them," but I didn't care about hiding my enthusiasm for the opportunity. I told them that I was 100% on board, and that I'd be up to Minneapolis within a month (adding that I'd be there earlier if they needed me).

When I thanked them for giving me this opportunity and ended the call, I felt entirely free of any kind of anxiety. I had spent most of my life planning for this moment, and it was finally here. My parents were the first to hear the news from me, and I paced around the house while excitedly telling them the details. The next day, I bee-lined to my supervisor's office at Garmin, politely thanked him for the employment there, and let him know that I was out the door in two weeks. Those last two weeks of fielding calls from confused GPS owners were oddly enjoyable, as I knew that every call was getting me closer and closer to doing something I actually cared about for a living.

In the two weeks between leaving Garmin and moving up to Minneapolis, reality inevitably set in. Yes, this was a huge and exciting opportunity, but it would also surely provide challenges for my anxiety disorders the likes of which I had never experienced before. My condition proved to be extremely difficult even when attending college or working at jobs that I didn't care about. Now I was faced with my dream job, and it was in a much more public role. Screwing up in that situation would devastate me far more than getting fired from some crappy TV station job because I had a panic attack while operating a teleprompter. I knew that challenges lie ahead of me, but I had no time to dwell on them considering I had mere weeks to find a place to live and haul all of my stuff up north. After many trips to Goodwill and a lot of Craigslisting, I managed to get rid of most of my bulky, unnecessary possessions.

Finding a place to live was a priority, but apartment hunting would be tricky considering I still lived in Kansas. My mother and I booked a weekend trip up to Minneapolis, and had a few apartments in mind to check out while we were there. Knowing that I didn't have the luxury of time when it came to this portion of the moving process, I signed on to the first place I visited. With a lease locked down, I went back home and spent the next couple of weeks saying goodbye to friends and family with a few "last hurrahs" at old stomping grounds.

Before I knew it, it was time to make the big drive. Since I was never a great driver even when I was behind the wheel of a standard-sized car, my mother and a friend of mine offered to drive the U-Haul behind me as we made the seven-hour drive up to Minneapolis. After spending the last month in a blur of excitement and preparation, it was my first chance to really sit back and think about what this meant for my life. I was leaving my entire family and social circle behind. Getting the job left me more excited than I had ever been about anything, but I was also being hit with more anticipatory anxiety than ever before. It was either going to be the greatest thing that could happen to me, or serve as evidence that my anxiety would get the better of me in big situations. I vowed to myself that the latter wouldn't be the case. Things wouldn't be easy at first, but I would do absolutely everything I could to ensure that this was the beginning of something great.

On my first day at Game Informer, I distinctly remember my heartbeat speeding up as I entered the lobby of their building. When I pressed the button for the fourth floor and the elevator doors closed, I remember taking one big breath before they opened again and I was thrust into my new life. I was nervous about every part of it. I worried about meeting with the new bosses. I worried about how often I'd have to speak in issue meetings. I worried about whether or not I'd have panic attacks while recording podcasts. I worried about how my bosses would react if I was open about my anxiety. All of these thoughts had been racing through my head for weeks, but I did my best to shut them out in that brief moment that I waited in the elevator.

The doors opened, and I walked in to meet the staff. I put on my best "I'm totally not nervous right now" face as Andy McNamara walked me from desk to desk and I shook hands with my new co-workers. Once that was done, he took me into his office to explain his plan for redesigning Game Informer's website. As he explained the new features and functionality of the site, I tried as hard as I could to focus on his words instead of the anxious thoughts that were bouncing around my brain ("It's not going to look good if I walk out of my boss's office on my first day as he's trying to explain something important to me," for example). I could tell that I'd have to eventually ask for reminders about what he had told me, but I was just happy to get through this first of presumably many anxiety-provoking events.

To my surprise, those first few weeks went fairly smoothly without any notable spikes in anxiety. An underlying nervousness stayed with me, but no more than most people feel whenever they're starting a new job or making a big life move. My first moment of severe panic at Game Informer came during my first issue meeting. With the entire staff gathered in one room, I immediately started worrying about whether or not I'd have to get up and step outside for a breather. As I normally did, I took the closest possible seat to the door in case things turned south.

Andy led the discussion about the contents of our next issue, and once again I found myself trying my best to pay attention to him instead of being up in my own head. Things escalated to a full-scale panic attack, which I hadn't experienced in months. Not wanting to leave the room, I sat it out. I did my best to take long, slow breaths, repeatedly reminding myself that it "it always ends." My bottle of water ran out and my mouth dried up, which gave me something else to be uncomfortable about. This attack lasted for close to half an hour, but it eventually peaked and (as it always did) ended. I sat through the rest of the meeting feeling like I could fall asleep at any moment, a common occurrence whenever my body would come down from a particularly bad panic attack.

Issue meetings became something I dreaded, which was made worse by the fact that I was now essentially scheduled at least one panic attack each month (only one if I was lucky). Rather than try to get out of them, I told myself I'd face my fear and sit through every one. Those training sessions at Garmin had given me similar attacks early on, but each one became progressively easier as it went along. I was in a better headspace now than I was back then, so I figured that I had already been through worse and came out the other side stronger.

Sure enough, each subsequent issue meeting was easier than the one that came before it. By the time our nearly all-day "game of the year" meeting came up at the end of 2009, I managed to sit through it all with mild to moderate anxiety. It only took a few months to get it down to those levels after having a full panic attack back in July. By that time a year later, I had almost no anxiety whatsoever during these long meetings, even when I had to speak.

Issue meetings were just one of the aspects of the job that I struggled with at first. The exact same progression of initially high anxiety, followed by gradual improvement carried over into podcasting as well. I had plenty of experience with writing (my primary role at Game Informer) before taking the job, but I had never recorded a podcast before. Predictably, it felt like second nature within a year of forcing myself to say yes whenever I was asked to be on one. Rather than dreading going into the studio, I actively looked forward to doing it.

One of the tougher elements of the job came from me doing video work. My resume listed the various short film awards, video production work, and live TV experience I had done in the past, but I got the impression that the bosses expected me to know more about high-end equipment than I did. All of my experience was either on my $300 consumer video camera that I bought at Best Buy or machines at the TV station that required me to follow very specific and fairly simple instructions to use.

Within a few months of starting at Game Informer, I had basically been picked to be the "video guy" for our monthly cover story trips to game studios. I was given expensive, high-end cameras that I had no idea how to operate, and the one person on staff that could have explained them to me would get visibly annoyed whenever I asked questions about them in an attempt to learn. Regardless of my inexperience with this level of video production, I was repeatedly sent out on trips as the only person responsible for video content.

The worst anxiety that came out of this situation happened during a trip to Seattle in January 2010. We were there to visit Bungie, the studio that formerly developed the Halo franchise. One of the many pieces of content that we'd be producing during the trip was a video interview with Marty O'Donnell, a well-respected composer who had worked on the series for years. We went into his recording studio and I started to unpack the large camera cases as the two writers I was with exchanged small talk with him.

I set up the tripod and put it in position, then I went to get the camera ready. When I took it out of the case, the lens piece completely separated from the body of the camera. It didn't make a noise or anything, so I hoped I'd be able to get it back on before anyone noticed what had happened. Getting the two pieces back together suddenly seemed like an impossible task as my anxiety spiked and my hands started shaking.

Within moments, I was deep in panic attack territory. As the small talk between the writers and Marty started feeling like it was going a little long, one of our writers glanced over at me with a face that read "aren't you supposed to be the video guy?" He reached out and grabbed the two pieces from me, and managed to get them back together with steady hands. I did my best to compose myself and shoot the rest of the interview with my heart feeling like it was about to burst out of my chest.

Doing projects with high-profile figures in the industry was a struggle for about a year after that incident. That summer, I was scheduled to interview Shigeru Miyamoto, perhaps the most famous video game developer ever thanks to his long history of creating classics like Super Mario Bros. and The Legend of Zelda. Normally, I'd have been relegated to the "video guy" role as someone else asked the questions. Considering how the Marty O'Donnell video went, however, I wanted to be in front of the camera as well in order to test myself further and get past this particular fear.

We arranged it so that one of our writers would be the one manning the camera, which should have been easy enough considering it would be a stable shot on a tripod. Ideally, I'd set everything up and hit the record button, and my co-worker would just stand behind the camera and make sure everything was operating correctly. As I'd be running to the interview straight from another appointment, my co-worker would be the one bringing the video equipment from our E3 booth.

Things seemed to start off on the right foot when I met up with Miyamoto and his translator. I was anxious to meet the creator of two of my favorite game franchises of all time, but I kept myself together as well as I could have hoped to. My co-worker showed up with the camera cases, and I started setting things up. Suddenly, I realized that a critical component was missing. I had asked him to make sure that he brought the shotgun microphone, but I didn't see it anywhere in the cases. He told me that he forgot it, and that immediately triggered a panic attack. Here I was, already trying to mentally prepare myself for talking to one of the biggest names in the history of the video game industry, and now I didn't know if we'd be able to get the video we needed for the site.

My hands predictably started shaking as I tried to scramble together some alternate solution. I landed on a less-than-optimal setup, but it at least did a good enough job to record usable audio. We only had a few minutes for the interview after I set things up, and I was even more frazzled than I normally would have been thanks to the pre-interview snafu. Despite how difficult it was and how much anxiety the situation triggered, I mentally put it in the column of "things that scared the hell out of me but I managed to pull through anyway." As that list grew bigger and bigger over time, it started making me significantly more confident to charge headfirst into new situations.

On top of the high-pressure interviews, another frequent source of anxiety came as a result of traveling to so many game studios and conventions. While much of the gaming industry was based in Seattle, San Francisco, Canada, and Japan, I was basically on an island in Minnesota. With no nearby studios, I had to fly every time I was on a cover story assignment. For many with chronic anxiety, planes are a surefire source of panic. Being on an airplane takes the anxiety of sitting in the middle of a packed movie theater row to the extreme. In the movie theater example, it's *possible* to step out and get a breather, it's just a pain considering you'd have to annoy everyone else in your row. When you're in a metal tube in the sky, there's literally no way to step out, get away from people, and compose yourself.

As a result, I decided that flying would be one of the few occasions that I'd use Xanax. For several trips in a row, I'd take half of a 0.50mg pill about 30 minutes before my flights, and it did have a substantially positive effect on my anxiety levels. After getting a few flights under my belt in this fashion, I started feeling better about the idea of trying it out without Xanax. Sure enough, I made it through the next flight feeling much better than I did when I had first started flying for Game Informer assignments. Each one after that proved to be easier and easier, as well.

One of the most consistent sources of anxiety (at least early on) was a weekly video show that I started with a couple of my co-workers. As I played an old PlayStation game called Twisted Metal at the office, I got into a fun conversation with my co-workers about our memories with it. One of my bosses came into the room and heard some of it, and said that we should go down into the studio and record us continuing the conversation while we played the game.

I grabbed some video equipment that I felt comfortable enough operating, and we went downstairs to record the first episode of Replay, which would become a weekly series that I eventually appeared on hundreds of times. Most people that watched my time on the show are probably familiar with me as a goofy, easily excitable personality as I played and watched these old video games. It certainly wasn't like that at the beginning, however. This first episode occurred when I had only been at Game Informer for about four months, and I hadn't yet gotten fully comfortable with appearing on podcasts and videos. I also wasn't entirely sure that I had set up the equipment properly. Perhaps most stressful of all was the fact that I'd be hosting the show, something that I had zero experience with. It was hard enough trying to keep my focus and respond to what others were saying, but I had never been the primary person responsible for keeping the discussion moving.

If you go back and watch the first episode of Replay (search for "Game Informer Replay Twisted Metal"), I sound considerably different than I did in later episodes once I had become comfortable with letting my personality out. Right out of the gate, I'm speaking way too fast, I stumble over my words on occasion, and I'm clearly not yet comfortable with letting my personality out very much.

Appearing on Replay, interviewing people, recording podcasts, attending issue meetings, and just about every other aspect of the job became easier every time I forced myself to face my anxiety and attack it head-on. As the years progressed at Game Informer, I travelled frequently and was a regular guest on the podcast. Virtually every week, I'd spend time in the studio recording the new episode of Replay. In every case of something that made me nervous about the job, I experienced improvement through repetition.

Throughout my life, I've always found that concept to be true. Improvement through repetition happens whether you know it or not. If you're a writer, your writing will naturally improve if you're producing consistent work whether it's for a multinational magazine or a personal blog that you haven't even made public. Malcolm Gladwell's book *Outliers* details how immensely successful groups and people like The Beatles and Bill Gates became masters of their craft after practicing them for over 10,000 hours. That "10,000-Hour Rule" applies on a much smaller scale, as well. The more you do something, the better you are at it, and my experience has proved to me that this concept works when it comes to anxiety-provoking situations. There are so many situations that I absolutely dreaded when I first encountered them, only for them to become complete non-issues after I faced them head-on over and over until it didn't faze me anymore. As of the writing of this book, I've appeared on thousands of hours of recorded media, traveled frequently (occasionally overseas), and have met or interviewed most of my idols in the world of entertainment. None of these situations give me anxiety any more.

Improvement through repetition is one of the early self-taught lessons that resulted in major reductions of my anxiety levels. As I got past these early hurdles, I wanted to start zeroing in on ways to eliminate every trace of anxiety in my life. No one with this condition can say they're ever fully "cured," but the steps I took in the following years effectively removed the vast majority of my symptoms.

A New Focus

Within the first year of working at Game Informer, I had turned almost every situational trigger for my anxiety into a total non-issue thanks to my "improvement through repetition" mindset. This was a major step forward for me, as there were almost no specific situations that I'd have to dread on a regular basis anymore (speaking in front of a live crowd remained one, but this wouldn't come up again until years later). That said, generalized anxiety disorder still managed to rear its head at unexpected times. The situational attacks brought on by panic disorder were reduced to rare occasions at this point, but it was time to figure out how to improve my overall health in an effort to combat the few remaining situational triggers and my unpredictable GAD.

I felt amazing once I started managing so much of my anxiety, and I knew that I was on the right track towards chipping away at the rest of it. There are no easy fixes with things like these, but I set off on several years' worth of decisions and habits that got me to the nearly anxiety-free life that I enjoy today.

Certain tactics and reminders have stuck with me throughout the years. I've already talked about "it always ends," "improvement through repetition," and attacking the things that scare me the most. Keeping those things in mind always helped, and I wanted new challenges to overcome since I had started conquering the work-related ones.

First off, the idea of tandem skydiving always scared the hell out of me. I had done solo static line jumps in the past, but mostly before my anxiety issues flared up. By 2012, it had been many years since I had last jumped out of an airplane and the prospect of doing my first tandem jump from 14,000 feet was terrifying. Because of how scared the idea made me, I signed up to do it.

For a solid two or three months, I'd have nights where I'd toss and turn in bed and worry about the jump. I was convinced that I'd have a massive panic attack during the plane's ascent, and it would cause a scene as the instructors would have to ground the plane to let me off. When the day finally arrived and I started watching the training videos and participating in the exercises, panic rose up in me in a way that I hadn't felt in months.

I put half of a Xanax pill in my back pocket for easy access, despite the fact that it had been a long time since I had last taken one. Every minute that passed by made me more anxious for the ascent, and I had to go into the bathroom to splash water on my face several times. I had gone skydiving before, but it had been so long and I had convinced myself that this would be the time that I'd have a massive panic attack. My friends were back in the hangar waiting for our plane to arrive on the tarmac, so I sat in a chair near the restrooms and did my best to breathe slowly and clear my mind.

It was here that I was oddly reminded of an old mindset that I used to have when I wanted to skip a class in high school. I distinctly remember one occasion in which I was sitting in a math class that had just started, and I wanted nothing more than to walk out and drive to one of my jobs at the movie theater or GameStop just to watch a movie or play a video game. After quietly packing all of my stuff into my backpack, I impatiently waited for the teacher to turn around or get distracted so that he wouldn't see me exit. Precious minutes passed by in which I could have been doing something more fun, and I was getting antsy. Eventually, I thought to myself "You're thinking too much about this. Turn off your brain and just do it." While the teacher could clearly see me, I stood up, walked out of the class, and drove to GameStop to play some new PlayStation 2 releases.

The moral of that anecdote isn't "hey, skip classes and play video games." What it was for me was one of my first exercises in something resembling mindfulness, whether I knew it or not. I cleared my mind of worries about the past or future, and acted on the present moment. When I was able to tell my brain to shut up its worrisome chatter for just a second, I was able to act on what I wanted.

Fast-forward to me sitting outside the skydiving airport's bathroom, and I suddenly remembered that thought from high school. "Turn off your brain and just do it." I stepped back onto the tarmac, took the Xanax out of my pocket, and threw it into the nearby grass. I wasn't going to voluntarily fill myself with anticipatory anxiety, I was going to get out of my own head and into an airplane, and then have a blast jumping out of it. The jump was amazing (search for "Game Informer's Skydiving Video" on YouTube if you want to see it), and the feeling I got when my feet hit the ground was similar to the feeling I had when I forced myself to run the teleprompter years earlier and got the job done despite fighting through intense anxiety.

A far safer (yet almost equally scary for me) proposal was public speaking. Back in college, my major required me to take either a public speaking or a philosophy class. I opted for the former, but dropped out after having a panic attack during my first speech. This, along with my anxious experiences with roll calls, the call center introductions, and having to speak up during Garmin training sessions and Game Informer issue meetings had left me with a nagging fear of getting in front of a crowd.

As I did with the fear of skydiving, I decided to be proactive about this particular situation. I looked around at local websites and eventually read about a bimonthly event called the "Drinking Spelling Bee" that was held at a nearby bar in Minnesota. I had always loved participating in annual spelling bees back in elementary school, and my post-elementary school self learned that I loved drinking beer. It was basically the perfect option for me – I'd get a chance to get a nice buzz going, face my fear of speaking in front of crowds, and take advantage of my skill in spelling to get free beers all night. Like everything else, stepping on stage at the bar to spell words into a microphone eventually became no big deal at all despite some initial anxiety.

Even after doing the Drinking Spelling Bee on a biweekly basis for a couple of years, I didn't feel completely prepared for an opportunity that came up out of nowhere. A local organization had started hosting "Nerd Nite" events in which experts on different topics would give a speech in front of a crowd about their areas of interest. I had gained a somewhat sizable Twitter following after several years at Game Informer, so the organization asked me if I'd be interested in being the show-closing speaker at an upcoming Nerd Nite. My first instinct was to say no, as giving a 10-15 minute speech sounded far more daunting than drunkenly spelling a word in front of a bar. Before I turned down the offer, I reminded myself of the mindset that I had been following for years now. This opportunity scared me, so I owed it to myself to go after it. Despite feeling overwhelmingly nervous, I accepted and started preparing my speech about how I got into the gaming industry. Overwhelming anxiety ran through me before I took to the stage, but I forgot all about the fear once I started talking and the speech went over far better than I could have ever expected it to.

Every time I ran into something that gave me that initial "uh oh, this might give me a panic attack" feeling, my mind went right to my old psychologist's story about the lady that was afraid to drop her groceries. My strategy of attacking these things was working. Instead of my world getting smaller thanks to avoiding situations that might give me panic attacks, my world was getting bigger thanks to my attitude opening me up to new experiences that I would have denied myself if I let my condition get the better of me. I was 100% certain that I was on the right track with anxiety management, and it was time to start getting serious about my overall health.

Part of me always knew that a regular exercise schedule would be invaluable for lessening my day-to-day anxiety, on top of introducing a ton of other benefits to my life. Hell, I experienced this firsthand when I lost thirty pounds and felt great during that summer in college. That said, I always saw it as a tough hurdle to jump considering my relative lack of athletic experience. I wasn't in college anymore, so I didn't have the benefit of a 24/7 rec center with a track and racquetball courts. If I wanted to get serious about exercise, I'd have to find other options.

I took a look at numerous gyms in an effort to recreate my extremely productive summer from college, but found none in Minneapolis that I could afford. Taking that same route wouldn't be an option, so I opened up to new ideas. Running on a track was out of the picture, so I decided to start running outside. It didn't take long for me to start loving it, as Minneapolis was full of beautiful running paths that went along the Mississippi River, through woods, and around the city's many lakes. Taking different routes for each of my long runs became something I looked forward to each weekend, and it really opened my eyes to how much of the city I wasn't even aware of.

As I got into the habit of running on a regular basis, I started learning new ways of motivating myself. Quantifiable progress was always something that I loved to see, so I introduced several ways of seeing my results in a clear manner. I downloaded an iPhone app that used GPS to track the statistics of my runs, and would frequently push myself to run as far as I could without stopping. Near the beginning of my interest in running, I'd hit a wall after one or two miles. Within a couple of months, I was regularly running more than seven or eight miles at a time without stopping. Being able to look at the history of my progress (as well as other stats) on my phone made me feel great about what I was doing and motivated me to continue to break my records.

I eventually doubled down on tracking my runs, buying a heart rate monitor and a wearable fitness tracker. If I looked at my tracking app at 10pm and noticed that I hadn't hit my daily goal, it always motivated me to go for a quick jog so that I'd get my numbers up. Graphs and numbers have always been extremely helpful to me, going back to when I confirmed the correlation between my hangovers and increased anxiety levels.

Exercising on a regular basis is just part of making major improvements to your health, so I started thinking more about my diet. I started making salads and bringing them to work for lunch, and implementing new thought processes when it came to how I ate. Whenever I got hungry, my mind would immediately start telling me to go get fast food, pizza, or something similarly unhealthy. In these moments, I started reminding myself of an obvious fact. I'd think "that [pizza/Taco Bell/etc.] sounds amazing right now, but the joy of eating it will be short-lived. The disappointment I'll feel after eating something so unhealthy will last a lot longer." I reminded myself that if I ate a salad or another healthy option, I'd be full at the end of the meal and feel great for the rest of the day thanks to making the smart decision.

With my mind focusing on my diet more than ever, I enlisted the help of another app to make it easier to form healthy habits. I downloaded a calorie-tracking app, and made sure to enter everything I ate on a daily basis no matter how much of a hassle it was. When I was able to clearly see how many calories I was taking in, it made it much easier to say no to that buffalo wing dinner or sixth beer if it was going to put me over my daily limit.

Plenty of modern technology was helping me track my day-to-day fitness, and I was feeling more motivated than ever. For the record, as of this writing I'm using Runtastic, Jawbone Up, 21K Runner, and

MyFitnessPal on a daily basis. I've tried a lot of different ones, and these have proved to be a great combination for running and weight loss management.

As I continued being cognizant of my fitness and diet, I predictably started shedding pounds and feeling healthier overall. It became easier to get out of chairs, to climb staircases, and even get motivated to get out of bed in the morning instead of hitting the snooze button. I also continued to teach myself new ways to keep myself in check when it came to my health. Having set goals always helped me, so I signed up for 5K runs and (later) 10Ks months in advance. Considering that these registrations usually cost $50 or more, I hoped that my frugal nature would override my laziness and keep me on track to be ready for them. After all, if I slacked on my running routine and couldn't run the race, it would be a waste of money. My assumption was correct, as having goals on the calendar kept me going more than a vague "stay in shape" attitude would have.

I was thrilled to find an affordable (free for the most part, actually) workout when it came to running, and it got me excited to try other forms of exercise to see if anything else would click with me. It didn't take long for me to take advantage of the great biking trails in Minneapolis, as I bought a bike and started going on long rides on days in which I needed to give my knees a break. I bought a Groupon for Muay Thai classes, and really enjoyed how demanding it was. It might have been a bit too much for a guy who's never been in a fight, considering I injured my thumb after just a few classes by throwing a punch wrong (the thumb still hurts when I bend it in certain directions to this day, so I haven't gone back despite my initial liking of the classes).

That Muay Thai injury actually opened me up to re-thinking long-standing avoidances that were tied to my anxiety. Despite going over a decade without taking medication for pain or sickness, I realized that I was being ignorant about that topic and started taking appropriate medication when needed (Ibuprofen for pain, cold medication when I was sick, nitrous during dental procedures, etc.). Sure enough, my worries about "feeling high" or anxious didn't apply when taking simple over-the-counter medication. I think I always knew that I was being unreasonable when it came to that avoidance, but anxiety can make your brain work in irrational ways.

I wanted to avoid giving myself excuses to not work out, as I started falling into the habit of not running whenever the weather was rough (which in Minnesota, it regularly was). My finances were what kept me from joining a gym in the past, but I changed my tune when I decided to make my health a priority. I couldn't afford a gym membership on my salary, so I cancelled cable and used those freed-up funds to sign up for a gym membership and run on their treadmills whenever the weather made it tough to run outside.

On one particularly nice fall day, I decided to go on a long run outside. My path took me around Lake Calhoun and the Lake of the Isles in Minneapolis, and I eventually hit my limit and got tired near the latter. As I slowed down and caught my breath, I noticed a bench near the water that I hadn't seen before. It was far enough from the roads and running paths, so traffic and pedestrian noise wasn't a concern. Sitting down sounded like a great idea after my long run, and it looked like a perfect place to relax and get a breather.

When I sat down, I was randomly reminded of meditation. It had been quite some time since I had actively practiced it, and in the back of my mind I was always wondering why I never pursued it more considering how effective it was. Sitting on the bench next to the lake, I figured there was no better time to give it another shot. My anxiety was lower than ever at this point in my life, but I assumed that meditation would still have some benefits. I didn't set my usual ten-minute alarm on my phone, opting instead to turn it off completely and just meditate until I didn't want to anymore.

Earlier in my life, I would have laughed and called you a liar if I told you that I'd thoroughly enjoy meditating on a bench next to a lake. It sounds so diametrically opposed to my personality, especially considering how quickly I used to dismiss such things as "a bunch of new-age crap" or "for hippies." Yet there I was, sitting on a bench with my shoes off as I focused on my breath and the sounds of the lake. To this day, I don't know if I've had a meditation session that drew me in so completely. I'm not sure how much time passed, but I remember being fully in the moment more than I had ever been. Outside thoughts weren't permeating my mind, and I wasn't internally counting down the seconds until I could stop meditating. I just sat, listened, and breathed in and out. When I finally finished (however long it took), I felt calmer than I had ever felt in my life. Even after my meditation session had ended, I just sat on the bench for a while and smiled at how amazing I felt in that moment. This thing that I would have quickly dismissed years earlier was proving once again to be something very real and very effective.

Meditation became a regular part of my life going forward from that day. I'd typically sit down for a session in the morning before I left for work, and it helped me feel more focused and calm throughout the day. At times, I'd also do it before bed. Insomnia had been a part of my life for as long as I could remember, but I found myself falling asleep within minutes of my head hitting the pillow if I had just finished meditating. Before meditation, random thoughts bounced around my mind endlessly as I laid in bed and tried to sleep. With just ten minutes of focused meditation, I found that I'd lay down with a clear mind that made all the difference in the world.

I meditated and ran throughout that autumn, but the latter became difficult to do once winter hit in Minneapolis. In the years that I ran while living in that city, my progress went back and forth like clockwork. I'd get in shape and work myself up to long runs, only to be forced to stop for months thanks to the brutal winters in the area. Once the weather made running possible again, I'd start back up only to feel like I was starting over from square one since I was out of practice.

For the winter of 2012, I decided that I'd need to find a new form of exercise that I could do regularly regardless of the weather. In the past, I had dabbled with the P90X video program and found myself surprised at how much I enjoyed the yoga days. Like meditation, yoga is something that I would have dismissed years earlier as "hippie crap," believing that it was tied to spirituality or "new-age nonsense." While there are certainly programs and classes that lean heavily toward that side of things, I was surprised to learn that there are many approaches that focus solely on the exercise component of yoga. P90X showed me that yoga could be an effective workout that's easy on the joints and could be done indoors with no equipment needed beyond a mat.

For a couple of weeks, I did the P90X yoga video daily. Needing something to shake up the repetition, I looked into other video programs that focused exclusively on yoga. I landed on DDP Yoga, a series hosted by former professional wrestler Diamond Dallas Page. When I first did it, I was pleased to see that there was absolutely no spiritual component whatsoever to the videos. With yoga being so easy on the joints, I was able to do it every day without ever feeling beat up or sore.

DDP Yoga was having a great effect on my health during that winter, and I decided to look into actual yoga classes so that I'd have something new to shake things up a couple of times a week. I found a yoga studio near my apartment that featured a "pay what you want" model, something that I previously didn't know existed. With the cost being so reasonable (I usually gave $5 or $10 per class), I had no excuse to not go.

My first class introduced me to an element of yoga that the video series didn't offer. Once we were done with the exercise portion of the class, the teacher instructed us to go into what's known as shavasana pose. "Pose" is used lightly here, as shavasana simply requires you to lay flat on your back with your eyes closed. In most other situations, this wouldn't do much. After an hour of holding poses and sweating through a class, however, it was immediately calming. Most teachers that I've gone to will dim the lights or play calming music during this portion of the class, which adds to the effect. As I continued to go to classes, I regularly looked forward to this reward at the end. "Laying down and closing your eyes" probably doesn't sound like that big of a deal if you've never been through a tough yoga class, but it was always the most relaxing part of my week once I started attending classes. It felt great physically, but it also had a positive mental effect as it reminded me that I had just spent an hour doing something so healthy for myself. These moments stood right alongside effective meditation sessions in terms of bringing about a relaxed state for me.

Yoga became something more than just an exercise that I could do during the winter. It mixed physical activity with a very calming, meditation-like effect, which couldn't have been a better combination considering the reasons I wanted to work out in the first place. Even though I always hated getting out of bed early (I usually got moving close to 10am on most days), I started looking forward to days in which I'd wake up at 5:30am so that I could get to my 6am class.

When the weather finally rose above "snot freezing" levels, I jumped at the chance to get back to running. That said, part of me dreaded it considering how difficult it had been in previous years to pick up again after several months off. In those years, I'd be lucky to finish a mile or two without slowing down to walk. Expecting a similar situation, I headed out for my first run of 2013 with the intent of seeing how far I could go. Over seven miles later, I was shocked at my ability to run that far without doing any running over the winter outside of the occasional treadmill session at the gym. Yoga had kept me in great cardio shape, and it had also been strengthening my leg muscles more than I realized.

The combination of running and yoga was perfect for me. I enjoyed both of them, and they complemented each other greatly. Whereas previous years frequently saw me taking time off from running due to leg/knee pain, the work I was doing with yoga was making my body more resilient and less prone to injury.

Despite working out on a regular basis and watching my diet, I was by no means some marathon runner or Mr. Universe candidate. That wasn't my goal, as my goal was simply to cut down on my anxiety levels. I always had some degree of a beer gut and was never a model of fitness, but the efforts that I was putting into managing my anxiety were having the nice side effect of keeping me under 200 pounds and feeling healthier on a daily basis. In the periods in which I slacked on working out, I put on weight, felt more tired, and had significantly higher anxiety.

Without realizing it, I was falling into (and sticking with) these healthy habits at the perfect time for my life. My next career opportunity promised to introduce no shortage of situations that would have likely been too much to handle if I hadn't learned how to manage my anxiety.

Ready For What's Next

When I started at Game Informer, it felt like the culmination of a career path that I had aimed for since I was nine years old. In many ways, the job lived up to what I hoped it would be. Deciding to leave the magazine and Minnesota wasn't an overnight decision by any means, but came rather from a steadily growing dissatisfaction with the company and an opportunity to work elsewhere that I had been considering for years.

With the Game Informer position came a degree of public exposure, and this grew over the years as I appeared on more videos and podcasts. Early on in my time at the magazine, two of my higher-profile followers came from another gaming outlet called Giant Bomb. Jeff Gerstmann and Ryan Davis first followed me on Twitter when I was professing my fandom for the much-maligned Nintendo character Waluigi, and my first interaction with Giant Bomb was an argument about this topic back in 2010.

Over the next year or so, I continued interacting with the two via Twitter. When 2011's E3 event was approaching, Ryan reached out to me to see if I'd be interested in joining them during one of their nightly podcasts. I knew their reputation for lengthy, conversationally loose podcasts, and the change of pace sounded fun to me. My nerves were high as I arrived at the house they were podcasting from, as I knew this would serve as my first impression to a new, larger audience. Once we started, I quickly felt at ease. The tone of the conversation was far more relaxed than what I had become accustomed to at Game Informer, and the fridge full of free beers certainly didn't hurt matters. Podcasting with Giant Bomb felt natural, and Ryan continued asking me to guest on the podcast during future E3 events.

A few months later, I was sent to a three-day review event for the new Call of Duty game. Jeff Gerstmann was there, and we spent a good portion of the event playing multiplayer with and against each other. As one of the nights was wrapping up, he approached me as I was heading back to my hotel room.

"I think I know the answer to this," he said. "But would you ever consider moving to San Francisco?"

He assumed that the "San Francisco" part of the question would be a deal breaker for me, and he was partially right. My first experience with the city had come while I was covering an event for Game Informer months earlier, and they had set me up in the Tenderloin district. This area was like nothing I had seen before in the Midwest, or anywhere else for that matter. People were smoking crack on the sidewalk in broad daylight, others were wandering in the middle of the street screaming incoherently, and I was harassed by more than one clearly disturbed individual during the block-long walk I had to make to meet up with my taxi.

That was my first impression of the city, and I incorrectly assumed that it was indicative of San Francisco as a whole. When Jeff asked me if I'd consider moving there, that initial visit to the Tenderloin was the first thing that popped into my mind. I was still mostly satisfied with my job at Game Informer at that point, so I told Jeff that a move was unlikely but that we should keep in touch.

As the years went on, I considered making the move to San Francisco more and more often. When I was assigned to cover other events in the area, I told Game Informer's travel people to place me in a hotel "anywhere but the Tenderloin." In doing so, I started experiencing more of the city and grew to like it more each time. I'd meet up with friends in the industry during these trips, and discuss my concerns about a potential move. I was happy to discover that several of my friends had made the move to San Francisco from other parts of the country and learned to love it.

More importantly, I was quickly becoming unhappy at Game Informer for a variety of reasons. At one point, I remember thinking that I'd be happier leaving the magazine and simply working for a bar or something simple along those lines. This book isn't the place to go into all of the reasons I wanted out, however. The important thing is that I was truly unhappy for the first time in a long time, and this feeling was ramping up exponentially as things got progressively worse at the magazine. Even with all of the positive changes I'd made in those last years in regards to my mental and physical health, it was hard to escape the cloud of negativity that I felt was

hanging over me whenever I was at work.
Considering that I had viewed Game Informer as my
dream job ever since I was nine years old, something
was clearly wrong and needed to change.

When Giant Bomb announced an opening for
their San Francisco office in early 2014, I knew that it
was time to make a big decision. Staying at Game
Informer would have been the easy, safe decision.
None of my duties there gave me any anxiety any
more, I had plenty of close friends around
Minneapolis, and it wouldn't be hard to just stay
complacent there and continue to write about video
games and collect a paycheck.

Staying at Game Informer would be safe, but
unexciting. Moving across the country felt risky, and
the prospect of starting from scratch in a new city
scared the hell out of me. I had always been good
about attacking whatever scared me when it came to
things like public speaking, skydiving, or getting used
to work-related duties like podcasting or appearing
on videos, but this was something different entirely.
This would be a completely new start in a mostly
unfamiliar city, and going to Giant Bomb would put

way more eyes on my work than what I was getting at Game Informer.

The thought of making the move made me as excited as it made me nervous, however. I wasn't being challenged anymore at Game Informer, as I had settled into my role and there were no more obstacles to overcome. After years of attacking the things that made me anxious, I started to thrive on that feeling of overcoming challenges that seemed daunting at first. Podcasts, video shows, travel, and writing cover stories filled that role during my early days at Game Informer, but they had become routine for me by the end. I looked at what Giant Bomb was doing, and they were appearing in front of 1,000-plus fans at convention panels, regularly producing podcasts that lasted over three hours, and spending tons of time in front of the camera. I loved the idea of this challenge, and their opening in San Francisco came at the perfect time.

I had come too far with my anxiety to surrender to the easy option at this point, so I applied to Giant Bomb and got the job. After receiving the call in which I accepted the position, I immediately informed Game Informer that I was leaving. I'd have one month to find a place to live, find someone to sublease my Minnesota apartment, and arrange to have all of my crap shipped across the country. More importantly, I'd have one month to get myself in the best possible headspace I could be in as I headed into this new challenge.

Without wasting any time, I doubled down on my meditation and exercise efforts. I ordered books on meditation, started doing both yoga and running daily instead of alternating between the two, went on numerous 30+ mile bike rides, and was more conscious about what I was eating than I had ever been before. I did my share of "last hurrah" nights with friends at my favorite Minneapolis bars and restaurants, but kept them in check enough to not derail my healthier efforts.

One of the books I read on meditation was called *10% Happier: How I Tamed the Voice in My Head, Reduced Stress Without Losing My Edge, and Found Self-Help That Actually Works*. It's by Dan Harris, an anchorman that's worked for *ABC News*, *Nightline*, and *Good Morning America*. It details a panic attack that he suffered while live on the air in 2004 during a national broadcast, and follows him beyond that as he learned about how to leverage meditation to combat his own anxiety disorders. His personal experiences with anxiety (and his search for ways to fight it) were incredibly similar to my own, and I was fascinated to read a story that I could relate to on so many levels. There are no shortage of useful books about meditation and anxiety disorders, but I wanted to draw special attention to this one considering how much of an impact it made on me during this time. If you find yourself relating to my story and are interested in hearing about the paths that others have taken in order to eliminate anxiety, I can't recommend it enough.

Reading that book made me even more motivated to keep up with meditation on a daily basis, rather than simply doing it when I felt like I had time for it. Meditation had proven its effectiveness to me on many occasions in the past, and it was time to make it a priority rather than something to do every once in a while. I started meditating for at least ten minutes in the mornings, and at least ten minutes before bed. During this month, I always felt alert during the day and was able to fall asleep quickly at nights. Both of those effects proved to be extremely helpful as I was going full-speed on trying to prepare for the move.

That month flew by faster than any I'd ever experienced, despite initially expecting it to feel like a relaxed, long vacation. The combination of preparing for the move and for the job had caused the days to become a blur, and before I knew it, it was time to jump in the car and begin the 30-hour, three-and-a-half day drive out west. My anxiety regarding driving on the highway would have to take a backseat for this period, as my excitement overpowered any other emotion that would have jostled for position in my mind's attention. It was almost a meditative experience to spend all of those days by myself, driving through South Dakota, Wyoming, Utah, and Nevada en route to California. I spent nights in Deadwood, Salt Lake City, and Reno before eventually pulling up to my new apartment in San Francisco.

Once I arrived in the city, I didn't have long to prepare for my first podcast at Giant Bomb. I finished the drive on June 29th, 2014 and it was time to record my first lengthy podcast the next day on the 30th. As I filled out my paperwork, I was pleased to discover that I wasn't having any anticipatory anxiety about the podcast that we'd be recording immediately afterwards. Years of being proactive about managing my anxiety, followed by a final month of really ramping up my preparation had done their job. Five years earlier, I would have spent my time in orientation fixating on my fast heart rate and attempting to control my breathing. In 2014, I was ready for this. All of that work wasn't just making my day-to-day life easier, it was also making sure I was prepared for my biggest life move to date.

Everything about that first day should have made me nervous. When it was time to podcast, I sat down in a professional studio instead of the unorganized closet I was coming from. I was about to podcast for far longer than I was used to, and it would be reaching far more people than ever before. Again, this would have been a recipe for disaster for the version of me from 2008. The 2014 version of me introduced myself and completed the recording with virtually no anxiety.

With Giant Bomb being far more video-oriented than Game Informer, I was prepared to be on camera or in front of a microphone during most days. Sure enough, I was being pulled into multiple videos or podcasts every day from my very first week forward. I made sure to keep up my exercise and meditation once I arrived in San Francisco, which I credit for my lack of anxiety from day one at Giant Bomb. If I had gotten complacent and slacked on those aspects of my life once I got here, I know that the anxiety would have snuck back up on me.

To this day (it's March of 2015 as I finish writing this book), I've had nothing beyond rare, brief, and minimal instances of anxiety during any Giant Bomb recording. Whenever my anxiety does start to creep up a little bit, my mindfulness practice has taught me ways to dismiss those thoughts before they ever flower into something more destructive. Thoughts that would have previously spiraled into panic attacks are now sputtering out upon arrival.

Appearing on podcasts and in front of a camera wasn't a problem in the least anymore, but it would only take a couple of months before my biggest challenge yet presented itself.

DAN RYCKERT

The Biggest Test to Date

Podcasts and videos were at least familiar settings for me from my days at Game Informer, but a new challenge was on the horizon that I hadn't attempted before. Giant Bomb's staff frequently appears at gaming conventions and speaks to auditoriums filled with more than 1,000 people. I knew about this before I took the job, and I expected it to be one of the biggest (if not the biggest) challenges of taking the position. Two months after I started at Giant Bomb, I was scheduled to appear on a panel at the PAX Prime gaming convention in Seattle. I'm sure that I could have explained my anxiety about public speaking to Jeff, and he would have taken me off of Giant Bomb's panel lineup if I requested. All of my experience up to this point told me that I shouldn't make that an option, however. I did tell him about my anxiety, but instead of asking to be taken off, I said "I want to be on every one of these until I get better at them and I get rid of my fear of them."

We were scheduled to do two panels at PAX Prime – one at a nearby bar that was only available to a couple hundred of our biggest fans, and the main panel in the big convention center auditorium on the next night. The smaller event would be streamed live on our website, and both panels would be recorded and available online soon after completion.

On the first day of the convention, we had a chance to explore the show floor and play a variety of games. At one point, I was scheduled to appear on my friend's panel that was being held in the same conference room as our big Giant Bomb one the next night. When I walked in, I was taken back by how huge it seemed. I had done the tiny Nerd Nite speech in Minneapolis and would be doing the bar speech later that night, but the size of this room dwarfed that of those locations many, many times over. While I had to appear onstage here for my friend's panel, I wasn't particularly anxious considering I'd just be playing a game with no real expectation of saying anything. It went by without a hitch, but I couldn't stop thinking about how many people would be packing that room at our panel just 24 hours later.

When we arrived at the bar for our smaller panel later that night, I felt at ease. We had a line of fans waiting outside, and I had a chance to talk to a lot of them before we took the stage. Being at a smaller venue made the panel feel less intimidating, and holding it at a bar meant that I'd have access to a little liquid courage if I needed it. Plus, speaking to a bunch of the fans ahead of time made it feel more like being in a room full of friends rather than speaking to a faceless crowd.

I had a few beers before the panel started, but I was largely sober when the cameras and microphones turned on. We sat in chairs on the stage as we discussed our site, its fans, and the games we had seen that day on the show floor. To close the show, we collected a bunch of fan questions in a hat and answered them. At no point in this process did I feel particularly nervous, and it made me optimistic for my ability to speak in front of the big crowd the next night.

Most of my next day was spent checking out games on the show floor and talking with fans, and I did my best to keep any anxious thoughts regarding that night's panel at bay. A couple of hours before our panel started, I felt the familiar tingling sensation in my extremities and noticed my breath becoming more shallow. It was nothing resembling a full-on panic attack, but there was no denying that I was about to face one of the biggest challenges for my anxiety to date. Each time I glanced at the hallway outside of our conference room, I noticed the line of fans getting bigger and bigger. They sat on the floor and played Nintendo 3DS games with each other, and I knew it would be no time at all until they were filling every seat in the Sasquatch Theater.

For some reason, I had assumed that we'd have beer or some kind of alcohol onstage with us. I was wrong, so I went downstairs to the bar and had a shot of whiskey right before the doors opened. One shot surely wouldn't be the difference between comfort and panic, but a little something to put myself more at ease didn't sound like a bad idea. I bought one beer to take with me and ran back up the escalator, hopping onstage just as the doors were opening up. As the fans started filing into the seats, I chugged water and chatted with my co-workers in an attempt to keep my mind from running wild with anxiety. I may have been in the best spot I'd ever been in my adult life in regards to my condition, but it's a condition that never fully goes away. This was a situation unlike any I had ever been in, and feelings of panic that had been dormant for months or even years were starting to rise up considering how inexperienced I was in regards to this particular stressor.

When the seats were all filled in, our microphones went live and Jeff started talking to the crowd to open the panel. I was amazed at his ability to talk to this huge room of people without any real scripting, direction, or noticeable nervousness, and I thought about how I'd love to get to that comfort level someday. For now, I just needed to make it through the next two hours. I didn't have to do much for the first six or so minutes, but it was my turn to speak up when Jeff asked me what games I had seen at the convention that day. Without much in the way of visible anxiety, I was able to get through a description of what I had played. Once my co-workers got into a longer conversation about a game they had both played, my mind started speeding up.

It's something I'd noticed plenty of times before. My anxiety would be at its worst in the moments leading up to the thing that made me anxious. It was always the drive to the TV station and the commercial breaks between running the teleprompter. It was in the times standing near the stage, waiting for the hosts to call my number at the Drinking Spelling Bee. It was the ascent in the airplane as we approached jumping altitude. It was never during the time spent actually doing the thing that made me nervous. When I was running the teleprompter, spelling my word onstage, or plummeting to the ground from 14,000 feet, my mind automatically became occupied with whatever it was that I was doing. In the moment, I never had time to worry about anxiety.

Likewise, I felt fine as I talked about the games I had played at the convention. Anxiety only crept up once the conversation moved away from me and I had time to get back up into my head. That's when the thoughts would bounce around at rapid speed – "When am I going to have to talk next? Am I being too quiet? I wonder if I'm visibly nervous...I feel like I'm doing the eye thing a lot. I'm running out of water really quick...what if my mouth dries up and I start having trouble swallowing?"

All of those questions eventually led to the thought that always popped up in these situations – "Am I going to have to get up and leave the room in the middle of this?" My symptoms were intensifying at a rapid pace, and I started assuming that I'd reach a breaking point and step out. I was already thinking about how I'd have to explain it. In my head, I pictured myself writing a blog post the next morning to be upfront with the reasons I excused myself (I hadn't yet talked about anxiety much on public forums).

Before those thoughts carried too much weight, I told myself that I was going to make it through the panel regardless of how intense my symptoms became. I reminded myself of the feeling I had when I drove home from the TV station after forcing myself to volunteer for teleprompter duty. If I stepped out, I'd feel brief relief followed by weeks of regret (and potentially a more intense fear of similar events going forward). If I stuck it out, I'd have to endure a very limited window of intense anxiety, but I could step away proud of myself at the end and more confident about appearing onstage in the future. Even in my rattled mental state, I knew what the best option was. Most importantly, I reminded myself that at no point in my twelve years of panic disorder had I actually had to get up and remove myself from a situation. I'd get through this just as I had hundreds of other situations.

Sure enough, I was a bit quiet during the panel as I weathered the storm of my first full panic attack in years. There are several times that you can see me becoming visibly uncomfortable, complete with eye twitches and water chugging. It picked up a bit at the end as the time approached to deliver a staged kick to my co-worker's face (for those not familiar with Giant Bomb, it's a long and weird story). If you're interested in seeing any of this, a search for "PAX Prime Giant Bomb 2014" should bring it up. At the panel, I was by no means as relaxed and talkative as I usually am in any of the projects I do daily at the office, but most people have told me that they didn't even notice anything was wrong. Even the worst panic that my body and brain could produce wasn't enough to result in anything worse than a somewhat quiet appearance. If it had become too much to bear and I had to leave, the absolute worst case scenario is that I'd write a blog post about my anxiety that explained what happened. It felt like the end of the world while it was happening, but a quick step back to think about the reality of the situation clearly shows that there was no nightmare scenario that could have come out of this.

After almost two hours of a sustained panic attack, the panel wrapped up and I immediately felt an intense wave of relief rush over me. A large portion of the crowd was waiting outside for the opportunity to chat with us and grab pictures and autographs, but that didn't worry me at all. Feeling thoroughly relaxed, I stepped outside of the theater and spent a long time meeting with fans. This was ideal for me at the time, as it gave me a great chance to be talkative and friendly to the fans that had just seen a reserved version of me onstage.

At some later point, I explained to Jeff that I had been fighting through a lot of anxiety throughout the duration of the panel. Despite this, I reiterated that I wanted to do as many of them as I possibly could. Whenever he was assembling a crew of Giant Bomb personalities to appear onstage in the future, I wanted to be a part of it so that I could continue to fight this one last big fear. He understood my reasoning, and put me on our panel for the PAX South event that would be coming up in January of 2015 in San Antonio.

In between the two PAX events, I put out a few tweets acknowledging that I had struggled with anxiety for quite a while. While I had been open about my condition for years with my friends, family, and co-workers, I rarely if ever mentioned it online. When I finally did, I started getting a ton of responses (publicly and privately) from Giant Bomb fans that told me that they struggled with the same thing. They told me that it helped to hear someone like me be open about these matters, and that they really appreciated it. It made me want to address anxiety more, but Twitter is where I have the widest reach and the format of that service isn't conducive to serious, lengthy discussions. I started considering writing a book, but couldn't decide if I wanted to put my full story out there in such a public manner.

I hadn't decided on what to do about this by the time I went to San Antonio for PAX South. Once there, my focus was on managing my own anxiety in the hopes that I wouldn't have a repeat of the panic attack at the first panel. Leading up to the new panel, I wasn't nearly as nervous as I had been in Seattle. Despite how rough that experience was, I pushed through and felt better immediately afterwards. I knew that I could do it again in San Antonio, I just hoped that my time onstage wouldn't be as tough to get through.

You can see this panel online as well (search for Giant Bomb PAX South 2015), and the difference between it and the first event is night and day. I'm relaxed, talkative, and didn't have any trouble being myself up there. A little bit of nervousness bounced around in me in the minutes before we went onstage, but it all went away once things got started. There wasn't any stretch of time in which I was worried about what I'd say or if I seemed nervous, and the panel flew by in no time at all. I stepped off the stage feeling great, and even more confident that volunteering myself for these was the right move.

Afterwards, it was time to do the meet and greets again outside of the theater. It was filled with the same type of picture requests and conversations that we're used to getting, but there was one big difference for me this time. At numerous points during the meet and greet, I had fans lower their voice a bit and pull me aside to tell me about their own struggles with anxiety. They repeated what I had heard on Twitter, saying that it helped to hear someone with a public persona be open about a struggle that they had personally experienced. It didn't take many of these stories to cement my decision to discuss my history with anxiety in this book.

Once I got back to San Francisco, I immediately started writing it. I went through old emails to my family, doctors, and teachers in which I wondered if things would ever improve. I found old journal entries that reminded me of just how impossible anxiety seemed to overcome when I was in the darkest points of it. Going through all of this really made it clear to me how far I've come in the last twelve years. I'm at a point now in which the only thing that carries the risk of a real panic attack is large-scale public speaking, and I feel like even that has been largely conquered. Writing this book and reliving the last twelve years in detail has almost been a therapeutic process, and it makes me even more confident that all of the decisions I've made over these dozen years have been positive and effective.

Three days before that PAX South panel, I ran out of my Zoloft prescription and didn't have time to get it refilled before the trip. I wondered if that would make my anxiety situation worse when I was onstage, but that clearly wasn't the case. As I had already been off the medication for a week when I returned to San Francisco and I had been feeling great for months, I decided to go off of it entirely. Going off of daily medication should be done gradually via a tapering process and with a doctor's supervision, but this circumstance didn't allow for it and it thankfully went well for me. My anxiety levels were at the lowest they'd been ever since before that first panic attack in the movie theater in 2003, so the time seemed right to stay off of the medication.

Less than a week before I finished the writing of this book, I appeared on two more large panels at the PAX East convention in Boston with almost no anxiety throughout them. One of the panels even involved me being the focus of a surprise trivia show that I had no prior knowledge of. This would have been an absolute nightmare scenario for me a few years ago, but I loved every second of it in 2015.

Rather than coast on my currently strong mental state, I decided that I'm going to continue to push myself forward even further. Physical health offers great benefits to mental health, so I signed up for a my first half marathon and have been training every week (and running a 10K and 12K in the time leading up to it) to get myself ready. I've continued to meditate for ten minutes every morning and every night, and just completed my first unbroken half-hour meditation session last week.

In addition to continuing the good habits that I've developed in recent years, I've also decided to continue being more open about anxiety disorders. I still maintain that Twitter isn't the place for serious conversation, but I've been more open lately via Tumblr, in-person talks with fans, and especially this book. Opening up to my close family and friends was a huge help early on in my struggle with anxiety, and it can only help myself and others if I'm open about it in more public forums.

As of this writing, I've had one panic attack in the last several years, and it was in a fairly extreme situation that doesn't come up often (the first PAX panel). This is a far cry from the daily dread and random waves of anxiety that plagued my college days and stuck around for years after that.

I've written plenty in this book about the habits, techniques, and reminders that have gotten me to the point I'm at today. I'll spend the next chapter running down the broad strokes.

DAN RYCKERT

The Rundown

If you're reading this book, it's likely that you're currently struggling with anxiety or have experienced it in the past and want to keep it under control. Now that you're well acquainted with the process that got me to where I am (mostly anxiety-free), this chapter will serve as a narrowed-down collection of the tips and reminders that have helped me along the way.

As I said in the beginning, I'm just a guy that talks about video games for a living. That said, I'm also a guy who's fought this thing for twelve years and it's all worked out pretty great for me. Instead of having all of the things that helped me spread out over all of the previous chapters of this book, I wanted to include a chapter that serves as an easy-access rundown for the tips that have been the most beneficial.

At the most boiled-down level, there are three pillars of my treatment that I point to as helping me more than anything – exercise, meditation, and attacking what scares you head-on.

Find an exercise that works for you.
Running and yoga turned out to be the key to getting me into exercise, but yours could be much different. Maybe you hate running, but weightlifting or martial arts are far more interesting to you. Find the thing that you actually look forward to doing, otherwise you'll be sabotaging your efforts by begrudgingly doing something where you'll just be watching the clock for the entire exercise.

If you can, use your knowledge of your own personality to do little tricks to incentivize the exercise. For example, I spent one recent night registering and paying for numerous upcoming races. I knew that it would drive me crazy to spend hundreds of dollars for nothing (races are generally non-refundable), so I signed up for all of them at once in the hopes that my cheapness would override my laziness. Sure enough, every time I feel like staying on the couch instead of running, I think "if I'm not ready for that half marathon, then I've wasted a lot of money." You know yourself well. Use that knowledge to your advantage.

Meditate. Mindfulness meditation has been a godsend for me when it comes to my anxiety as well as my daily thought processes. It's easier for me to focus on the task at hand, it gives me more energy, it helps me sleep, and (most importantly) it lowers my anxiety by teaching me how to keep destructive thoughts from lingering around my brain.

This is a difficult one to start, and everyone sucks at it at first. You *will* find your mind wandering. You *will* finish sessions without feeling like you were able to maintain focus. That said, no meditation session is useless. It's called a practice for a reason, and like anything else, you will improve over time through repetition. I tried to complete a thirty-minute session for years before I was finally able to get it done for the first time a few weeks ago.

Start with something relatively easy. Tell yourself you'll do it for ten minutes every day, and you can choose when that is (I'd recommend either the start or the end of your day). Set an alarm for ten minutes, and do your best to focus on your breath for the entire duration. When outside thoughts wrestle for your attention, acknowledge them and let them float away without giving them the time of day ("I'll deal with that thought later when I'm not meditating" is a good attitude when that happens).

If you have trouble focusing on your breath, try other methods. Try counting each breath, and starting again from zero if you catch your focus drifting to something else. Do a body scan, and focus your attention on each body part in sequence from the bottoms of your feet to the top of your head. Search YouTube for guided meditations (after all, my first meditation in Buddy's psychology class was very much a guided meditation). If you find yourself uncomfortable while sitting cross-legged on the floor, consider trying a meditation pillow.

There are a ton of different ways to practice meditation, and many books focus specifically on the "how-to's" of each kind. I don't intend for this book to be an instruction manual for how to meditate, I just hope that it points people towards learning more about the practice. Check out *10% Happier* as a start, then visit any number of websites that focus on mindfulness meditation (or any other form of meditation you'd like to explore) for tips on beginning your practice.

Attack what scares you. Remember the lady in the grocery store? She was terrified of the mundane act of going grocery shopping, but quickly overcame her fear by confronting it head-on. If you're anxious about socializing at a work party, don't use that as a result to skip it. Instead, show up on time and force yourself to make it through. If someone from your class has to present a project and the idea gives you anxiety, don't lay low and hope someone else takes the lead. Speak up and be the first to volunteer. If sitting in the middle of a movie theater row scares you, get there early to make sure you're as enclosed as possible. It'll be rough for a while, but you'll leave the situation feeling like you've conquered something you fear.

Keep in mind that all things should be considered from a safety standpoint first and foremost. Going to a work party, presenting a project to your class, or sitting in the middle of a movie theater row can't hurt you. If you're terrified of driving on the highway and you know that it'll give you a panic attack, don't volunteer to drive into rush-hour traffic right away. Start small with something like driving on a rural highway with little traffic, and gradually work yourself up as you build your confidence.

If I hadn't attacked the things that scared me, I'd have missed out on many unforgettable experiences. I wouldn't have accepted jobs at Game Informer or Giant Bomb, I wouldn't have gone skydiving with my friends, and I wouldn't have travelled to any number of game studios or conventions. My life would be drastically different if I hadn't charged into anxiety headfirst, and it would have certainly been for the worse.

Those are the three main pillars that have helped me escape years of near-constant anxiety, but they're not the only lessons to be learned from my experience. Here are some others.

Be open. Feeling like you don't have anyone to talk to about your condition makes it far worse. If the idea of opening up in person is overwhelming, start on an anonymous mental health message board that focuses on anxiety. Another good option is finding a therapist that specializes in patients with issues similar to yours. When you're ready, talk with those closest to you about what you're going through. Beyond that, you may find it helpful to let your boss or coworkers know about it. That certainly helped me, as everyone would know what was happening if I had to step out of a meeting for a quick breather.

Discover connections. Learn about the different situations that tend to be tied to your anxiety levels. For me, it was the nights of extremely heavy drinking. When I made those charts in college, there was no denying the direct correlation between a wild night and a panic-filled next day. If you notice yourself consistently becoming anxious during or after a particular activity, it's in your best interest to be aware of that connection and keep it in mind before you partake in it. If you know that caffeine is a trigger for your anxiety, you have no one to blame but yourself if you're feeling bad after your fifth Mountain Dew of the day.

Don't expect to be "cured." It's not going to happen. Anxiety is a chronic condition, and even those that have gotten through the worst of times are susceptible to the return of generalized anxiety and panic attacks. I'm feeling better than I have at any other point in my life without a doubt, but I have to remind myself that the anxiety can come back. This is a benefit towards my overall health, as it keeps me vigilant when it comes to exercise and meditation schedules. If I lower my guard and decide that I've overcome my condition, I risk slacking on meditation, exercise, and the attitudes that have gotten me to this point.

Strike a balance. "Everything in moderation" applies to so many things in life, and I found that to be the case with anxiety treatment as well. Going out and partying could turn into a terrible next day if I went too wild, but I learned ways of going out without the anxious side effects. All it took was finding that balance, and this is different for everyone. By graphing my alcohol/anxiety levels in college, I learned that 10+ beers in a night would result in a rough tomorrow every time. That said, I found that I could still go out and have a good time with five or six beers, but without the strong anxiety the next day. As it's different for everyone, you need to listen to your body when it comes to this. If one or two beers is enough to trigger panic attacks, you should probably consider cutting alcohol out entirely.

I know that I'd be healthier overall if I never went out and got drunk with my friends, but it's something I've always enjoyed doing. By finding a way to do this while still avoiding anxiety, I've found that balance that works for me. Striking that balance is important, and it can keep you from going too extreme in one direction.

Avoid crutches. If you're turning to a substance or destructive activity to soothe your anxiety symptoms, that's not healthy. This applies to a wide variety of crutches, from legal escapes like alcohol and junk food, to more extreme examples like harder drugs. Even prescription medication can become dangerous if used as a crutch. If I ran to the Xanax bottle every time I felt a tinge of anxiety, dependency and addiction could have become very possible side effects (in the case of prescription medication, always consult with your doctor if you notice your habits changing).

I'm happy with my current balance of alcohol in my social life, but I'd have a much different opinion on the matter if I ever found myself rushing to alcohol in an attempt to soothe my symptoms. I don't see much harm in a couple of drinks before a rare situation like the PAX panels I wrote about, but I'd have to seriously assess the situation if I found myself taking shots at home because I felt some generalized anxiety coming on.

What determines if something is a "crutch" is wildly dependent on the person, but that's likely what it is if you find yourself running to it at the first sign of anxiety. Keep an eye on these things and determine if they're helping your efforts or hurting them, and respond accordingly.

Set quantifiable goals. If you tell yourself you're going to do vague things like "eat healthier" or "exercise more," it can be hard to remain motivated. Taking a day off can turn into taking a week off, and before you know it you're back where you started. When it comes to exercise and meditation, I found that it always helps to set a clear goal. By giving myself a target weight or a target accomplishment (the half marathon), it always gave me something to measure my progress by. When I started running, I'd frequently tell myself "I'm going to run as far as I can in this direction, and keep going until I can't run anymore." The next day, it would feel like a victory even if I ran one or two houses past my previous attempt. Seeing progress before your eyes, whether it's a physical landmark or the number on the scale can be a huge motivating factor.

Make your recovery a driving force in your life. If your anxiety is getting to the point where it's the hardest thing you're dealing with, then making progress towards alleviating it should be your top priority. Nothing is more important than your mental well-being, as it determines how much you can enjoy every aspect of life. Events in your life that should be happy can become trying ordeals if you're not in the right mental space, so attack anxiety with everything you've got.

Don't worry about "normal" anxiety. If you're going through a major life change (moving, getting a new job) or have a really important or intimidating event coming up (a speech, a job interview), it's normal for *anyone* to be nervous. It's by no means indicative of your diagnosed anxiety conditions causing more trouble for you, it's just a normal human reaction to these situations.

Explore options. The methods in this book are just a fraction of the possible approaches you can take towards improving your situation. Read other books. Try new forms of exercise. Talk to friends and doctors. Give things a chance even if you may be initially skeptical of them. Sometimes it'll turn out that you had a reason to be skeptical, and other times you'll stumble upon effective methods that you love. I may not have found St. John's Wort or acupuncture to be helpful to my cause, but I approached yoga and meditation with the same level of skepticism and discovered two of my favorite activities.

The magic potion doesn't exist. Overcoming anxiety is a complicated process with no surefire solution for anybody. Certain mindsets and reminders can help tremendously, but every person has to find their own path towards recovery. I wanted that magic cure back when I first started struggling with anxiety, but the long path to where I'm at now proved to be far more rewarding than any quick solution. Make it your mission to overcome your condition, and don't waver in the face of difficulty. Every panic attack ends. You can either make your world smaller by avoiding the situations that scare you, or you can face them head-on and come out the other side a stronger person.

DAN RYCKERT

Anxiety as an Ally

It's taken me twelve years, but I can say with confidence that I'm finally where I want to be. I wish I could have said that when I got my first "dream job," but my anxiety made it hard to be fully in the moment and enjoy everything to the degree I should have. Anxiety can be an albatross that brings down every aspect of your life, or it can be a driving force for making you a better person. You can choose which direction it takes you.

I think about what my life would have been like without this struggle with anxiety, and I genuinely believe that I would have been worse off. If anxiety didn't give me the drive to charge headfirst into scary situations, maybe I would have been complacent to work at a job that I wasn't passionate about. If I didn't have anxiety to make me look into exercise and diet options, I could have easily said "I don't like working out or watching what I eat" and gradually slid into obesity or poor overall health. If I opted to stick to the "safe option" of sticking to writing at Game Informer, I wouldn't have displayed a personality on videos and podcasts that eventually led to my employment at Giant Bomb.

I've come very far since that first panic attack on January 1st, 2003. That said, anxiety will always be a part of my life. I still involuntarily twitch my eyes around a bit when I'm on camera or when I feel myself getting nervous. I still eat slowly at restaurants and almost always have to take half of my meals home with me. I still have an ever-changing level of beer gut, and I haven't been able to shake a lifelong love of the most unhealthy kinds of fast food. I'll still get butterflies before I have to get on stage in front of large crowds. There's still work to do, but these are such small issues compared to the omnipresent dread and frequent panic attacks that hounded me for so many years.

I'm glad that I still have these reminders that there's work to be done. They'll drive me to continue my improvement in every area, from eating better to setting new goals for my physical fitness. In having a defined enemy to defeat, I have something to fight for. If I didn't have to worry about the return of generalized anxiety and panic attacks, I wouldn't be signing up for that half marathon or eating that salad instead of a plate of buffalo wings. I haven't had my last panic attack, and that reminder is what keeps me motivated to improve myself.

Turning my condition into a force for positive change has been a key factor in the happiness that I feel every day. Even if modern science invented that magic pill that could take away the threat of anxiety for the rest of my life, I wouldn't take it. So many of the great experiences in my life have come directly out of my fight against anxiety, and I honestly consider the condition to be one of my life's greatest allies as a result.

You can let anxiety defeat you, or you can use it to bring out the best version of yourself that you can possibly be. You make the decision whether you want to make your world smaller or if you'd rather push yourself to do things that you had no idea you were capable of. Your path towards recovery will be unique to you, but persistence, a positive mindset, and a determination to improve can overcome anything anxiety can ever throw at you

Acknowledgments

Going back through twelve years of ups and downs, old emails and journal entries, and plenty of memories to produce this book has been a tremendously rewarding experience, and I want to thank the people that helped make it possible:

- Justin McElroy, Jason Berger, Phil Kollar, and Casey Malone for their proofreading and feedback.
- My family for being there for me even if they didn't fully understand my condition at first.
- All of my friends, bosses, and teachers who have been supportive and patient when I've been going through tough times.
- Buddy, the University of Kansas psychology professor that introduced me to meditation.
- Every fan that has approached me at conventions to discuss their own anxiety issues.
- Luke Smith for his fantastic work on the cover.
- Jeff Gerstmann for his support of my side projects, and for continuing to put me on panels to help me overcome the fear of public speaking.

If you're struggling with anxiety yourself, I hope that this book has been of help and reinforces the fact that you're not alone.

Made in the USA
Middletown, DE
11 December 2015